THIS BOOK is to
commemorate the issuance of the
official Florida Seminole medal
September 15, 1973
and is limited to 15,000 copies

No. 10225

Photograph by John I. Grif

SEMINOLES often still live in traditional *chickees* well-adapted to the distinct environment of the Everglades with its frequently windy expanses of water, shown in this contemporary view on one of the Florida reservations.

THE FLORIDA SEMINOLE PEOPLE

by Charles H. Fairbanks

Scientific Editor: Henry F. Dobyns
General Editor: John I. Griffin

PUBLISHED BY INDIAN TRIBAL SERIES / PHOENIX

Library of Congress Catalog Number 73-87997

PRINTED IN THE UNITED STATES OF AMERICA – Imperial Lithographers

VIRGIL N. HARRINGTON

THIS BOOK IS DEDICATED TO Virgil N. Harrington, retired former Superintendent of the Florida Seminole Agency and Area Director at Muskogee for the U. S. Bureau of Indian Affairs. The esteem in which Indians hold him is eloquently conveyed in the following appreciation written by a tribal chief in the Muskogee Area:

"Virgil N. Harrington was in the vanguard of those who changed the very image of the Bureau of Indian Affairs from an autocratic, dictatorial management agency to that of a technical advisory service.

"This is true because he possesses a compassionate heart saturated with the milk of human kindness for those he served for some three decades as a U. S. government official.

"He epitomizes all that was good and kind and noble to a confused and frustrated people who had for untold years faced both a hostile environment and a peculiar fusion of paternalism and dictatorship on the part of their U. S. government master. In short, Harrington brought a new and long over-due breeze to the Bureau. He helped to change its image in the eyes of the First Americans whose lives he touched during his long and laudable career as a servant of these defeated and hapless people."

VIRGIL N. HARRINGTON

[C]HAIRMAN OF THE FLORIDA SEMINOLE TRIBE, HOWARD TOMMIE.

LIVING IN SMALL SCATTERED CAMPS in the Florida Everglades and the Big Cypress Swamp are the Florida Seminole, perhaps the least changed and least known of any American Indian tribe. Their colorful costumes of patchwork and the claim, which many Seminoles still maintain, that they never signed a treaty of peace with the United States make them of extreme interest. For over two hundred years the Seminoles remained isolated from the growing society of southern Florida. Only within the last few years have they begun to participate in the rapidly expanding economy of the state. How the Seminoles moved into the state during the early part of the eighteenth century and rapidly adapted to successive living spaces and environments is a fascinating story that can only now be described in any detail.

The final adaptation of the Seminoles was to the great "River of Grass", they call "Pahokee".

Ecologists describe the Everglades as a wet, semitropical savannah, a flat wet land, fertile if drained, but strangely for the Indians not immediately hospitable. They had to learn over many years how to live and exploit such a new environment. Today much of the Everglades is protected by the great Hoover dykes around Lake Okechobee, and by numerous drainage ditches. Once drained, the rich black muck soil is incredibly fertile and produces great quantities of vegetables which find their way to homes in the entire eastern United States. Where it has not been drained and planted it presents a nearly flat vista of green or yellow grass, broken here and there by single or numerous cabbage palms. More widely scattered, on slightly higher parts are "hammocks" or dense growths of live oak, and many more tropical trees foreign to the rest of the United States. From the air it presents a rather desolate spectacle, while from ground level it gradually assumes an enchanted aspect of grass, palms, broken occasionally by the darker masses of live oaks. Travel is difficult. In earlier times only the shallow dugout canoes of the Seminoles could readily traverse it. Now air boats and marsh buggies with towering tires can go almost everywhere. Widely scattered throughout the Everglades and the somewhat less open Big Cypress Swamp are the camps of the Seminoles, now seemingly fully at home in this strange land.

Photograph by William D. Boehmer

JOSIE BILLIE WORKING ON A TRADITIONAL STYLE Seminole dugout canoe in the dense growth of the Everglades. He fashioned this canoe for the Smithsonian Institution.

EARLY TRIBES

The Seminoles were not, however, the aboriginal inhabitants of Florida. They are recent migrants from the north who assumed possession when the original inhabitants had been destroyed in the face of European settlement. These original Floridians were thickly scattered over the entire state. In the south were the Calusa, a fierce hunting and fishing group who never accepted Spanish authority with any permanency. To the north were the partly agricultural Timucua, and to the west the fully agricultural Apalachee. Archeology has amply demonstrated that these various groups and their ancestors had occupied the land for long periods, perhaps back to the end of the Ice Age when Florida teemed with big game. The Apalachee and Timucua were part of the Spanish mission system and were subjected to the ravages of diseases introduced by Europeans to which they had little or no resistance. This, along with occasional revolts, brought about a sharp decline in their numbers but their final disappearance was caused by slaving raids from South Carolina. Beginning in 1702 Carolinians began a steady series of raids into Spanish Florida. Destruction of the Mission Indians was rapid and by 1711 there were no organized Indian towns in Florida except in the immediate vicinity of St. Augustine where the great Castillo de San Marcos offered some protection from English raids. In St. Augustine itself these Indian remnants began to be assimilated into the Spanish population. Florida had never developed a firm resident population of farmers and craftsmen as it was an almost purely military settlement. During the first half of the 18th century, Indians were welcomed to St. Augustine and the native population there actually increased while the rest of the state was becoming almost completely depopulated.

Northward in Georgia Emperor Brim of the Creeks was building a dream of driving the Europeans out of the New World. His master plan called for a first attack on the South Carolina settlements. The resulting war, known as the Yamassee War for the Creek allies in Carolina, was short, nearly successful, and set the stage for the repopulation of Florida. In 1716 the Georgia Creeks, most exposed to the possibility of retaliation by the Carolinians, began to move away from Central Georgia. The Spaniards, realizing the advantages to be gained, encouraged Creek Indians to move into the area formerly occupied by the Timucua and Apalachee. Two principal areas of settlement developed, one near the present Tallahassee in former Apalachee territory, the other near present Gainesville in what had once been the heart of the Timucua country. The Indians in both areas came largely from central Georgia and spoke dialects of the Hitchiti language. Hitchiti is part of the larger Muskogean Family of southeastern Indian languages, spoken by most southern tribes with the exception of the Cherokee. One of these new towns, perhaps the most important was Mikasuki, a few miles east of Tallahassee. Through the years the name of this town and dialect has come to be used to refer to the older, more numerous language group of the Seminole. Only recently has Mikasuki been studied by linguists and reduced to written or printed form.

THE SEMINOLES EMERGE

The Spaniards began to refer to these new Indian migrants into Florida as "Cimarrones", meaning "Wild Ones," because they moved into wild, unoccupied territory and were thus distinguishable from the Indian remnants settled in the vicinity of St. Augustine. The Creek or Muskogean languages contain no sound corresponding to English "R". Thus, the Spanish Cimarrones became to the Indians, "Semilones", soon changed to Seminoles, and the new migrants acquired the name they bear today.

While the Spaniards had actively sought the movement of the Creeks into Florida, they seem to have had few formal dealings with them once they had arrived. The Spaniards in Florida had developed the mission system for controlling

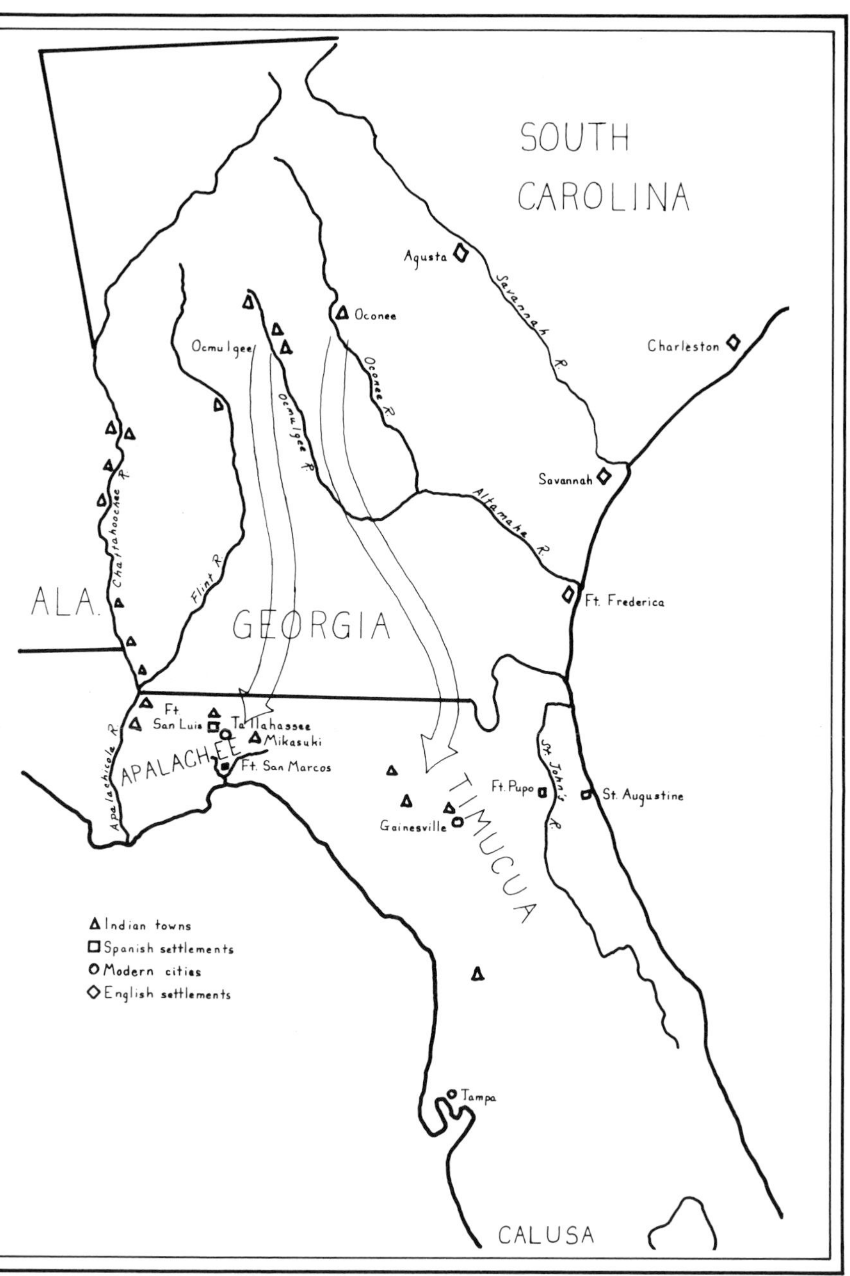

AP 1. Spanish Florida Prior to 1763

and using Indians in their colonial system. They had never developed the trading system in use by the English and French colonials as a means of extracting products from the Indian country. During the early years of the Seminole occupation of Florida there seems to have been little formal contact between the bulk of the Indian population and Spanish authorities. Occasional parties of Seminoles journeyed to St. Augustine for conferences, but their major contacts with Europeans continued to be with Georgian and Carolinian traders. The basis of this interaction was the trade in deer skins, a major source of leather in Europe at that time. The Spaniards never did develop any regular system for supplying the needs of the Indians for European manufactured goods. Especially reluctant to supply the Indians with firearms, the Spaniards in effect forced the Indians to maintain some relationships with the English traders.

This need for the European products to which refugee Indians had become accustomed was one of the factors which gradually changed Creek culture into Seminole culture during the 18th century. The Florida Seminoles also had to adapt to changed climate and differing local situations. While the agricultural system remained basically the growing of corn, beans, squash, and tobacco, they began to plant sweet potatoes, melons, and other crops borrowed from the Spaniards. Growing seasons were different and soils were generally the sands of Florida, much lighter than the tough red clay of the Georgia piedmont. They also began to use intensively the herds of wild cattle that had multiplied, especially in the Alachua area, after the destruction of the Timucua missions and the Spanish ranches located there. The chief of the Alachua settlement was known as Cowkeeper, and beef became an important item in Seminole diet for the first time. Wild oranges had spread out from the Spanish settlements and the Indians learned to appreciate them eaten with sweetening of wild honey. These changes were accompanied by changes in the style of their houses, villages, and certainly many other aspects of their lives.

One of the important changes was their gradual sense of separation from close involvement and control by the Creek national system of Georgia and Alabama. Most of the Creeks who moved to Florida did so as small bands, probably only parts of towns. Thus they found it difficult to establish the strong town organizations which had been so important a part of Creek political structure. They did maintain the clan system and the basic forms of the religious pattern which was closely related to the family and political forms. Smaller settlements, however, and their hunting of wild cattle made necessary a much simpler town political system than had been customary in Georgia. The ties with the rest of the great Creek Confederacy were beginning to dissolve. They were settlers in a wild, deserted country, far from the settled towns of their kind and were involved in a struggle to adapt to new environmental conditions. Perhaps the fact that they were now the possessors of a new name, Seminoles, was an added factor in this separation.

Spanish control and possession of Florida was by no means strong or vigorous and in 1763 Spain was forced to relinquish the colony to Britain. The British colonial authorities were at that time engaged in a determined effort to organize their relationships with the various Indian tribes on the colonial borders and had developed a pattern of signing definitive treaties with the Indians. At the Treaty of Picolata they had hoped to secure a cession of lands, roughly the northeast quarter of Florida from the Indians. The Seminoles did meet with the British officials in company with their kinsmen from the Lower Chattahoochee River towns, but the principle chief of Alachua, Cowkeeper, developed a diplomatic illness that kept him away. When the other Indians had returned to Georgia and Alabama, Cowkeeper appeared, showing as well as any European treaty negotiator that he had independent status, must be treated separately, and given a separate treaty medal. One major effect of the English dominion in Florida was the establishment of several British trading

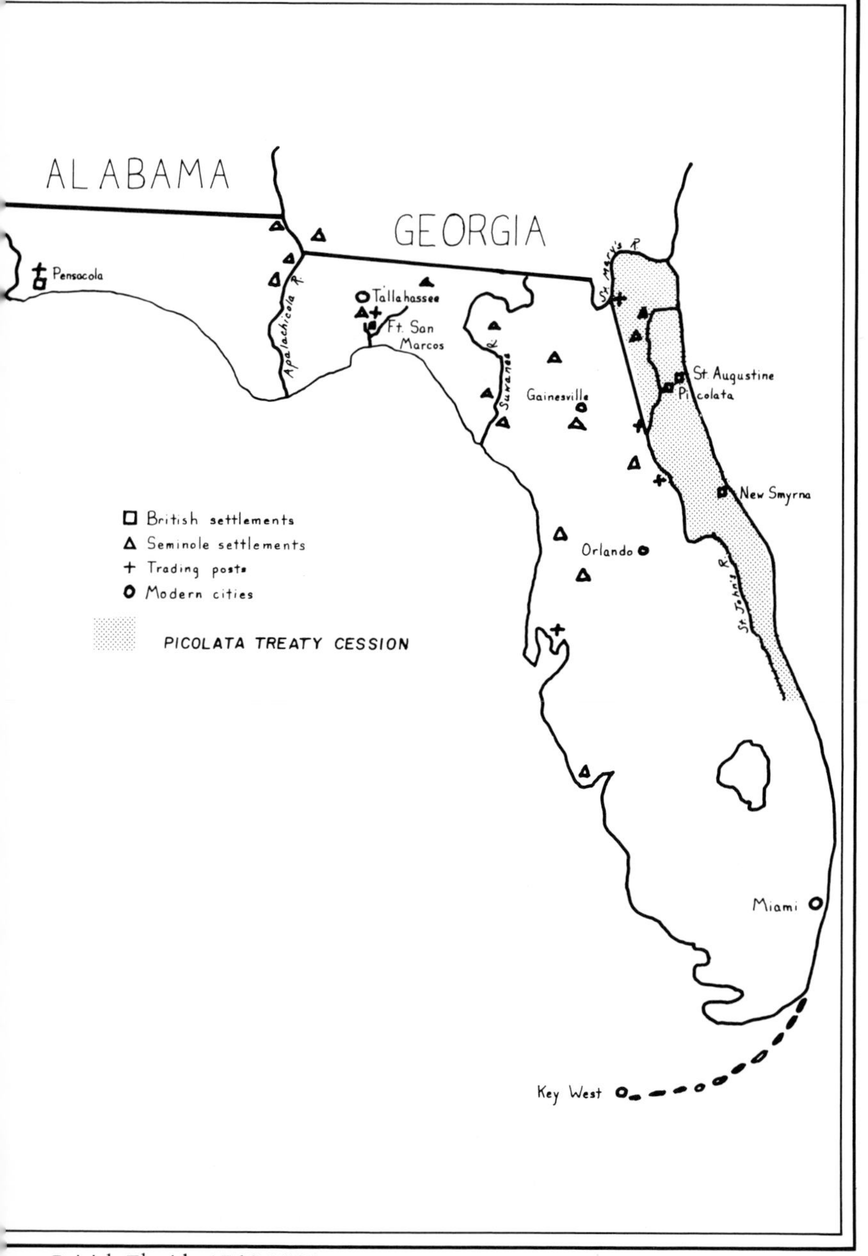

P 2. British Florida 1763-1783

posts in Florida. Into these establishments came the Indian products: great numbers of deer and wild cattle skins, and a few furs. From them spread such products as guns, iron tools, cloth and a variety of personal ornaments. Among the items of jewelry glass beads were the most abundant, but silver earpendants for both men and women were also popular, as well as mirrors, red paint, and crescent shaped silver neck ornaments. The trade was by barter with the prices quoted in deer skins and no actual money changed hands. As the products the Indians had for trade were largely the products of men's activity, and the majority of the goods they received in exchange were useful to men, the importance of men was paramount in the trade. As a result, the male aspects of Seminole and Creek culture changed more during this period than did those spheres of women's influence. Home life still centered around the matrilineal family and child rearing. Women's crafts such as basketry and pottery remained unchanged.

As early as 1700 Florida had been a refuge for runaway slaves from the Carolina colonies to the north. With the settlement of Georgia the number of escaped blacks increased even more. The Spanish authorities were generally reluctant to return these people to their English rivals to the north. The Spaniards developed at least one settlement of blacks near St. Augustine and generally used them as farmers and occasionally

Courtesy Smithsonian Institution National Anthropological Archives

THIS PHOTOGRAPH taken around 1890, Billie Stewart (r.) wears silver gorgets ıich had much earlier become traditional among many Southeastern Indians. The minoles and other tribesmen copied these elements of European military uniforms the 17th Century. The gorget derived from the neckpiece of body armor, but came ornamental on officer's uniforms after armor became obsolete. Seminole en fashioned their gorgets from silver coins hammered thin. This photograph by ıarles Barney Cory, Sr., shows Stewart and Tony Jumper (l.) wearing turbans pical of the final decade of the 19th Century. Their long shirts, deerskin leggings, d mocassins are also characteristic of Seminole styles at that time. Their crossed ger-woven sashes with long fringes which end in feather tassels are also typical of e Seminole and other southern tribes.

as soldiers. With the development of increased Seminole settlements in the interior of the colony, many Negroes fled there rather than to St. Augustine. The Seminoles were generally quite permissive to these runaways, rarely holding them as personal servants. Instead the blacks generally formed separate towns near and under the sponsorship of the Indians. Many Negroes served as advisors to the Seminoles in positions of trusted aides. While little intermarriage took place, there did develop a system of mutual trust and interdependence between these two groups of refugees from the dominant white culture to the north. The Seminole emerged as the protectors of the Negroes and often prevented northern slave-catchers from recovering the refugees. In the 19th century this was to become an even more important aspect of Seminole life.

As the most recent British colony in North America, and because of its isolated position, Florida was not involved in the American Revolution to the extent of the more northern, older colonies. Thus the Seminole were not involved to any extent in the fighting on one or the other side that characterized the Revolution for other tribes. Florida was in fact a refuge for loyalists from the other colonies and saw the development of numerous plantations raising cattle, indigo, sugarcane, and other crops. None of this seemed to affect the Seminoles and their continued development as a somewhat separate element of southeastern Indian culture continued. At the end of the American Revolution the Treaty of Paris returned Florida to Spanish rule in 1783 and most of the British inhabitants moved to still loyal colonies. What did remain to mark the passing of English dominion was the cession of a large bloc of land in northeastern Florida from Indian to European title. Yet the very Treaty of Picolata which conveyed the land also was to serve as a recognition of Seminole rights to the rest of Florida. Another legacy of the British Period was the series of English trading posts that had been established to serve, and partly to control, the Seminoles. The Spaniards realized that the most effective way to control the Indians was to supply them with trade goods. As Spain could not supply these herself, she reluctantly agreed that British nationals could remain in the colony on a temporary basis. This interim arrangement lasted until the final departure of the Spaniards. While the trading posts presented a major element of control, they also created problems for both the Indians and the Spaniards, or the Americans for that matter. Rum had been a consistant element of the trade for Indian goods with all the problems that it created among a people not really used to distilled alcohol. The trade also was largely conducted on a credit basis with the Indians securing supplies in advance of the hunting season of the winter months. Somehow the Indians never managed to secure enough skins to balance their previous purchases. The result was an accumulating mass of debts to the traders. Some of these were eventually discharged by cessions of lands to individual trading companies. Such was the great Forbes purchase of nearly 1,000,000 acres in western Florida which settled debts of both the Seminoles and their kinsmen the Lower Creeks.

THE CREEK WAR

As the 18th century drew to a close the Seminoles were beset by a number of problems. Spanish administration of Florida was increasingly weak. Settlers in southern Georgia presented a constant source of friction. British intrigues along the southern coasts added complications to their existence. Early in the 19th century the Creeks of Alabama felt an increasing pressure from Americans on the east in Georgia, on the north in Tennessee, and on the west in the newly acquired Louisiana Purchase. In addition a treaty with the United States allowed pioneers transit through the Creek country to reach the new lands in the west. The result was inevitable, the Creek War of 1814 in which Andrew Jackson was to win much of the fame that eventually took him to the presidency. When the Creeks lost the war, many of the leaders of the revolt fled to Florida as it was foreign soil and they had kinsmen there among the Seminoles. These new additions to the Florida populations were mostly Upper Creeks from central Alabama who spoke the Muskogean tongue. Once again it was a case of Indians unwilling to submit to white domination who migrated to Florida. Their numbers added a substantial increment to the Seminole population, perhaps as much as the Seminoles already there. Many of them simply found homes in already existing Seminole towns. Others moved through the earlier settlements and founded new towns or camps in the central part of the Florida peninsula.

While the Seminole Nation thus became a people of two distinct languages, there seem not to have been any other big differences between the two groups. While the Mikasuki and Muskogean languages are distantly related they are regarded as mutually intelligible by the Seminoles. Today many members of the tribe can understand and use at least a few words of each language, everyone considers himself a speaker of one language or the other. The Mikasuki are regarded as the least willing to adopt white ways, and do in fact preserve more of the old ways. The basic differences within the tribe, however, seem to relate to where one has lived and how conservative his family was during his early years. From the early 19th century onwards the Seminoles have been a group with two separate languages, but a common culture. Rivalries between language groups do not seem to have developed to any extent, perhaps because of their common front of opposition to whites.

The First Seminole War was a direct outcome of the situation in Florida at the beginning of the 19th century. Spain was very weakly administering her colony and American frontiersmen were eagerly trying to develop a pretext that would assure that Florida became American. Border incidents involving cattle or horse stealing occurred with increasing frequency. As tension between the fledgling United States and Great Britain increased the southern frontier was inevitably to become part of the conflict. Americans, concerned about the integrity of their borders, saw Florida as a logical extension of their dominions. England used the southern coasts, poorly defended by Spain, as a base for clandestine operations. At least one British agent, William Augustus Bowles, was a flamboyant adventurer who had a strong following. Encouraged by the receipt of arms and ammunition from the British, the Seminole began to take a tougher stand against white frontiersmen. When British agents began drilling Indians and Negroes in the streets of Pensacola, Andrew Jackson marched on the town and captured it. There was little point, however, in fighting the British on Florida soil in 1814 and

Jackson marched on to New Orleans and the bloody finale of the War of 1812. This was not to end the troubles of the Florida Seminoles, although it did give them a respite.

THE FIRST SEMINOLE WAR

Soon border incidents began to mount. Surveyors trying to run the international boundary between the United States and Florida encountered determined resistance in the Seminole part of the line. A more serious incident occurred on the Apalachicola River, at the extreme western edge of the Seminole settlements. There the British agents had constructed a fort, at first garrisoned with both Indians and Negroes. After the departure of most British agents, the fort was mostly occupied by Negroes. When United States forces tried to move supplies for Fort Scott in southern Georgia up the river they were strongly attacked from the fort. Retaliation was immediate and an American gunboat sailed up the Apalachicola River, in Spanish territory, and totally destroyed the fort. This whole incident was regarded as a perfect opportunity for the United States and Andrew Jackson again led an expedition into Florida. In 1817 the border incidents had reached a pitch that could only be settled by further hostilities. Late in 1817 American troops attacked the Seminole village of Fowltown near the American line. British agents were again involved and had supplied at least some arms and much encouragement to the Indians. The American troops under Jackson and Gaines were ordered to attack south of the border in Spanish territory. Jackson was willing to occupy all of Florida if the President would support such a move. While the Indians certainly resisted American encroachments, and were encouraged by British agents, it is clear that the United States badly wanted Florida and was ready to use almost any excuse to get it.

Jackson's raid into Florida started at the old Negro fort on the Apalachicola and rapidly moved eastward through Tallahassee to attack Mikasuki. Fort St. Marks and the nearby settlements, inhabited largely of recently arrived Creek refugees from Alabama, were taken in short order. From Fort St. Marks, Jackson marched eastward to the Suwannee River as the Indian groups scattered at the approach of the Americans. Along with some refugee Upper Creek leaders, Jackson captured and executed two English traders whom he accused of being spies and of inciting the Indians. Jackson then turned his attention westward and briefly occupied Pensacola. The inability of the Spaniards either to control the Indians and the British agents or to prevent the depredations of the Americans in her territory set the stage for the diplomatic negotiations that ceded Florida to the United States. The Adams-Onis Treaty of 1819 transferred Florida to the United States

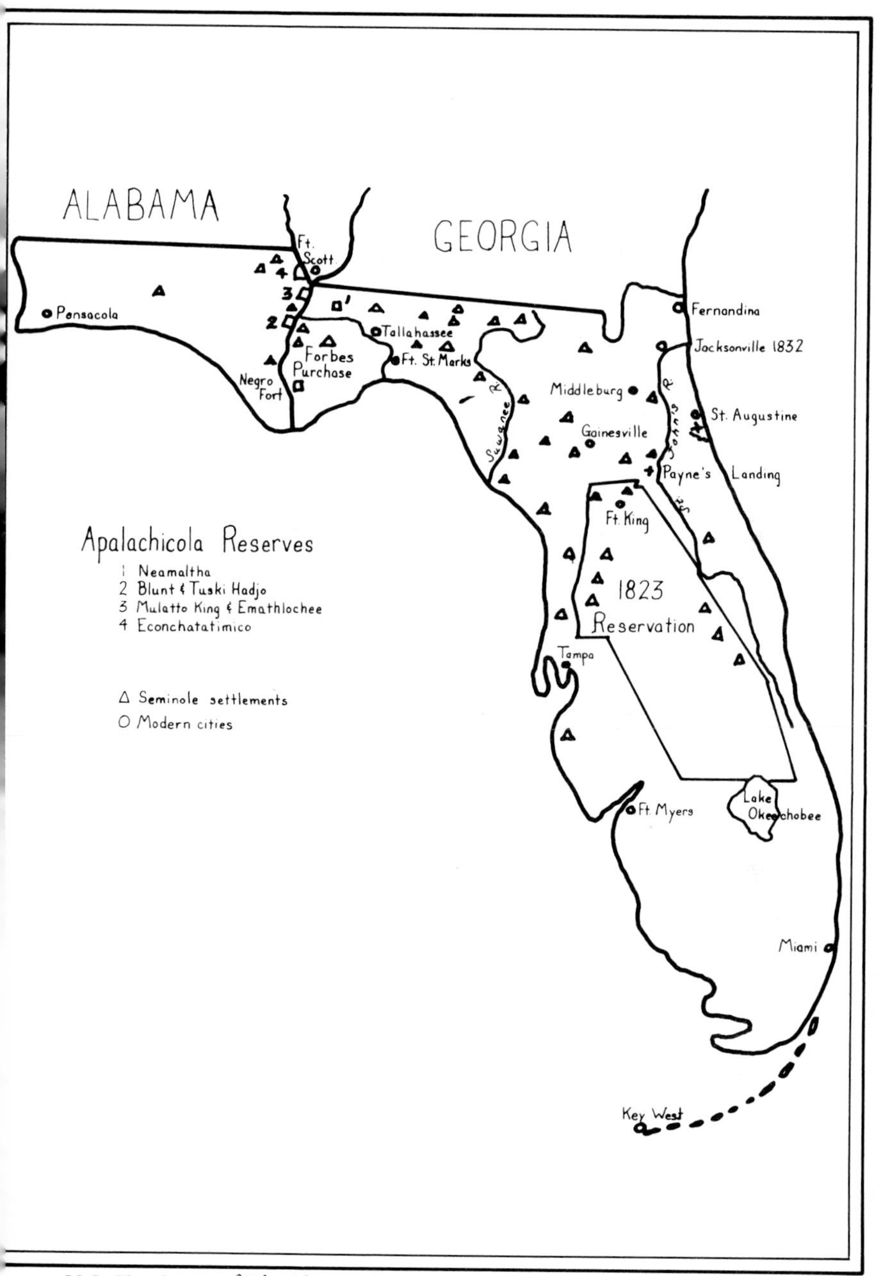

AP 3. U.S. Territory of Florida 1819-1845

for the consideration that the United States would assume payment of claims by frontiersmen for depredations caused by the Indians. It was not finally ratified until February 22, 1821.

THE AMERICAN DOMINATION

When Florida became territory of the United States, St. Augustine and Pensacola were the only Spanish settlements of any size. The rest of the area was unknown even to the Spaniards. The Seminoles were quite numerous, mainly in the northern parts of the territory. About 5000 Indians were about equally divided between Mikasuki and Muskogee speakers. Towns were scattered from the Apalachicola eastward to the St. Johns and southward to the vicinity of present Ocala. A few Seminoles had penetrated as far as the head of Tampa bay, but the southern part of the state was completely unoccupied. While some of the larger towns had family homes built around a square ground for religious and political meetings, the more usual pattern was of scattered family homesteads. This form of settlement suited the need for dispersal in the face of attack and fitted the combination of farming, hunting, and fishing activities by which the Seminole subsisted. In many respects it resembled the scattered frontier farms of the whites who were eager to encroach on Seminole territory.

TREATY OF MOULTREE CREEK

From the beginning the U.S. territorial authorities realized that it would be necessary to establish some sort of working relationship with the Seminoles. The Indians were invited to Moultree Creek, near St. Augustine, in 1823 for the purpose of signing a treaty. On September 18th some thirty-two chiefs signed the treaty which provided that the Seminoles give up all claims to Florida lands in exchange for guarantee of perpetual rights to a reservation in the center of the state. Various other clauses provided for an annual payment of $5,000 each year, one year's food supplies, and that the Indians would apprehend and surrender all runaway slaves. Secret provisions gave small grants of land along the Apalachicola to chiefs who had assisted in getting the treaty approved. The reason given for locating the reservation in the center of the state was that it would make difficult Seminole contact with whites and thus reduce tensions. It seems likely, however, that this land was considered of little use to the Territorial and federal authorities. Much of it was scrub land, now verdant with citrus groves, but not of much use for Indian agriculture. It is archeologically quite vacant and evidently never has been a suitable place for large numbers of Indians.

The signing of the treaty was followed by a

period of rising tensions. The food supplies promised were slow in coming and of inferior quality. As territorial lands were surveyed and sold to settlers increasing friction developed as the often starving Indians killed cattle and made other depredations. The provision that runaway slaves would be surrendered by the Seminole was viewed by many whites as a license to catch any blacks that could be found whether or not they could be identified as runaways. In view of the mutual trust that had developed between Blacks and Seminoles, this was a continued source of stress. Fort King was established near present Ocala as the headquarters for the Indian agent provided by the treaty. The early agents seem to have understood few of the problems facing the Seminoles, or perhaps just did not care. Territorial governors meddled in Indian affairs and there was a rising sentiment throughout the United States that all eastern Indians should be moved to new reservations west of the Mississippi. The Seminole just wanted to be left alone without any contact with whites, so forced migration was not an attractive solution. They believed that they had rights to Florida by settlement and conquest. In addition they did not want to be forced into close relationships with other southern tribes, many of whom had fought against them in the First Seminole War. In 1832, some Seminole chiefs were persuaded to sign an agreement at

Payne's Landing to send a delegation to Oklahoma for the purpose of inspecting the land set aside for the Seminoles. While in Indian Territory the chiefs signed another agreement to remove all Florida Seminoles to the new home picked for them. Many Seminoles viewed this as an act of treachery because the tribe had no formal, overall leadership. Each village had a chief or series of chiefs, but no tribal head was acknowledged. At the earlier Treaty of Moultree Creek they had informally agreed that Neamathla would be their spokesman. No other chief was ever given the right to deal for all the Seminole towns. One young chief, Osceola, was especially outspoken against any dealings with federal or territorial authorities. Osceola had been born in Alabama and was a nephew of Peter McQueen, one of the Red Stick leaders in the Creek War. Having fled to Florida at the close of the war, the band in which Osceola was traveling was intercepted but later released by Jackson's forces. Childhood memories of harassment by Jackson's troops were now coupled with fresh instances of injustice to make the young Osceola one of the most determined enemies of the whites. The paper signed in Oklahoma gave the Seminole until 1836 to move and Osceola began to object strenuously to any such event. The inevitable result was war – The Second Seminole War.

Some Seminole town chiefs planned to accept the orders to move and began to assemble at Tampa bay for the trip. Osceola killed one such chief, Charley Emathla. The federal authorities sent a body of soldiers from Tampa to reinforce the garrison at Fort King. The Seminole chief Alligator ambushed them in what became known as the "Dade massacre" after the officer in charge of the troops. On the same day Osceola led an attack on the headquarters of Ft. King, killing the agent and several others. Early in 1836 Micanopy, a venerated chief, sent word that he was tired of war and asked for a parley. While the parley was going on other troops fired on the Indians, killing a number while Osceola escaped. The United States was not prepared to fight a war of the Indians' choosing in the swamps and forests of Florida. Local militia and regular troops were often completely bewildered by the Indian techniques of raiding and then fading into the forest or swamp.

In spite of the general lack of U.S. success, the Indians were ready to move to Oklahoma, realizing that they could not long fight the armies that the United States was assembling in Florida. When they began to assemble at Tampa they learned that they would be settled among the Creeks who had recently been removed from their remaining lands in Georgia and

Courtesy The Charleston Museum

OSCEOLA, PAINTED IN CHARLESTON a few days before his death on January 30, 1838, became the national hero of the Seminole people because of his resistance to U. S. removal policies during the Second Seminole War. Born in Alabama around 1804, he came to Florida with other Red Stick refugees at the close of the Creek War. He led the attack on Ft. King that started the Second Seminole War in December, 1835. Captured by the forces of General Joseph M. Hernandez under a white flag of truce on October 21, 1837, Osceola was first imprisoned at Ft. Marion in St. Augustine and then removed to Ft. Moultree, South Carolina. Having been ill for some time with malaria, he died soon after arriving at Charleston. The attending physician removed his head as a souvenir.

Alabama. Memories of Creeks with Jackson in First Seminole War were still too strong for this to be very attractive. Slavers also began claiming many of the Seminole Negroes as escaped slaves. As a result of these factors, Osceola and many of his supporters fled Tampa in the night and the war resumed its dragging course. Gradually both the Indians and the war moved southward until fighting took place in the vicinity of Lake Okeechobee, where the federal troops were completely frustrated by the terrain of the Everglades. Osceola, and eventually some thirty other leaders, were captured while parleying under a flag of truce. When some Seminole chiefs were imprisoned in the old Spanish fort at St. Augustine, they escaped by starving themselves until they could slip through the high, narrow Spanish window. Osceola, imprisoned at Ft. Moultree, South Carolina, soon died in prison, when his head was removed as a souvenir by the attending physician.

The Second Seminole War dragged on until 1842 in a series of futile efforts on both sides. The Indians gave up in small bands and were shipped to Oklahoma, where once again they had to learn to adapt to new conditions. The War has been estimated to have cost the United States some $40,000,000 in expenses, the destruction of property, and loss of life. Nearly 1,500 regular troops met death at the hands of the Indians or through disease in the unfamiliar climate. At its peak the United States had nearly 9,000 men in the field while the Seminoles could never muster more than 1,500 fighters, and were never able or inclined to put that many into one action. Not until the 1960's was the United States to fight again such a frustrating tropical war of attrition against such odds of disease, heat, and an enemy who was unwilling to fight the conventional war of the textbooks.

While the bulk of the Seminole who survived the war were gradually moved westward, the irreconcilable core of the resistance withdrew into the unexplored wastes of the Everglades. There they could not be found by the army, or if found, could not be caught. Finally the United States simply abandoned the contest leaving a few Indians, probably less than 300, hidden in the Everglades. This remnant represented a doubly distilled band of Indians who had a long history of withdrawing from contact with the whites. First in the 18th century when their ancestors had left Georgia, and again when the bulk of the tribe had eventually gone to Oklahoma, these were the hard core that once again moved into new and unfamiliar country to escape cooperation with the whites. They were truly Seminoles, "Wild Indians" living in a wild but strangely beautiful country.

They faced many problems in adapting to the entirely new environment of the Everglades. The extremely small size of the total population and

SEMINOLE MAN POLING A DUGOUT CANOE, photographed about 1910. Hewn from a single cypress trunk using adzes and axes, the Seminole canoe with its long pole was ideally suited to cross the marshy expanse of the Everglades seen in the background

Courtesy Smithsonian Institution National Anthropological Archives

'he tall grass grows in a few inches of water most of the year. The numerous rivers nd slews provide somewhat easier traveling ways. Wilson Cypress is here wearing the ld type of man's "big shirt".

the impossibility of finding any reasonably large plots of dry ground, coupled with the need for secrecy, produced a pattern of small isolated camps, each under the leadership of a woman who formed the nucleus of the local band. This pattern of strong maternal ties that they had inherited from their Creek ancestors seems to have been strengthened in this period. The small size of these family camps made it almost impossible to maintain the tribal or even the town political forms of an earlier day. Land suitable for agriculture was scarce and scattered, and new methods of tilling were needed if they were to survive. The land did, however, abound in plants, animals, birds, and fish that could sustain life if they could learn the proper methods of collecting them. The Seminole did learn to survive in that new land and their numbers began to very slowly increase.

THE THIRD SEMINOLE WAR

They were not however, to be left alone. The few settlers in Florida thought that the Indians should be removed once and for all. In 1853 Congress passed an act forbidding any Indians to remain within the state of Florida. An agent was hired to persuade them to leave, presumably peaceably. At a cost of some $53,000 some 36 Indians were in fact transported to Indian Territory. Even the far away Congress felt that this cost was excessive and the project was dropped. Friction continued, nevertheless, and the frequency of incidents quickened. In 1855 a surveying party deep in the Big Cypress Swamp found a field of corn, beans, pumpkins, and bananas. Using what they wanted and destroying the rest of the surveyors greeted Bowlegs' objections with ridicule. Chief Bowlegs returned the next day with allies and in the resulting fire-fight the surveyors were severely wounded. Both federal troops and State militia were brought into the resulting Third Seminole War. Like the earlier war, this was inconclusive with army troops unable to find the Indians in the Big Cypress and the Everglades. Some 41 were eventually captured and an unknown number killed in the next three years. Finally the Secretary of War had a delegation of Oklahoma Seminoles brought to Florida who were to persuade the Indians to emigrate in return for various moneys. Some 123 Indians accepted the terms, leaving an estimated 300 still in possession of their homes in the Everglades. From this final nucleus has grown the present Seminole Nation of some 2,500 persons.

The troubles of the Seminoles were not over, although they were never again actually to wage a war against the United States. In the 1880's and again about 1900 incidents occurred that seemed to the few white residents of south Florida to presage another Seminole War. In most cases the whites seem to have caused the

GROUP OF SEMINOLE INDIANS IN CANOES, Miami River, about 1902. A few bands of very early patchwork can be seen on the costumes. This group was probably visiting one of the trading posts in the Miami area. The short triangular cape on the back of the man's shirt was typical of the period. For much of the southern Florida

Courtesy Smithsonian Institution National Anthropological Archives

ırea canoes were the major means of transport. The art of hewing canoes from :ypress logs is old among the Indians of the Southeast. The Seminole adopted the ›ointed bow from European types and developed a light, shallow boat that could :ross the Everglades with ease.

problem by willful disregard of Indian rights or by sheer unwillingness to allow the Seminoles to remain in the wild existence they so strongly cherished. South Florida was beginning to be settled. Ft. Lauderdale and Miami had been established and some traders were supplying the Indians with increasing amounts of goods. These consisted of: pots and pans, traps, guns and ammunition, cloth, canned goods (especially canned peaches), flour, grits, salt, axes, hatchets, saws, hammers, and large quantities of nails. Jewelry consisted of many glass beads and watches, watchfobs, and the like. In exchange the Indians offered egret plumes as long as the taking of them was legal, pet animals, alligator hides, baby alligators, corn, pumpkins, beans, blueberries, wild grapes, chickens, and alligator teeth. A special product was the "Koonti" starch made from the root of the Sago Palm. This trade seems to have been conducted for cash by most of the trading posts. The Seminole began to use the word "shuto-cuna-waw" the old word for "stone beads." The Seminoles were beginning to adapt to a money economy, at least in their relations with the whites. Most of the trading posts were some distance by canoe or ox cart from the camps deep within the Everglades where the Seminole chose to live.

Much of Florida was quite unknown to the outside world and Seminole served as hunting guides in the interior. They also began to act as cowboys for the cattle ranches then being established on the grassy plains of the Kissimmee Prairie and the northern parts of the Everglades. The romance of these unconquered Indians was also beginning to attract the attention of some persons. Clay MacCauley reported on the Seminoles living north of Lake Okeechobee and some popular books brought them to the general attention of the world. The virtual isolation that the Seminoles had enjoyed after the Third Seminole War was beginning to disappear. The Federal government began to assume some responsibility by the purchase of lands for reservations in Broward, Martin, Collier, and Hendry Counties. Previously to this time the Indians had been living on private or state lands without any real title to their camp sites and garden plots.

SEMINOLE RESERVATIONS

The United States considered that the Treaty of Payne's Landing in 1832 had extinguished the Seminoles' claim to the reservation in central Florida. The Seminoles who refused to leave Florida thus had no legal reservations for nearly a hundred years. In 1950 the Seminole Indians of Florida filed a petition under the Indian Claims Commission Act to recover compensation because their original title to Florida land was extinguished under duress. The claim has proceeded to a decision favorable to the

Seminoles on May 8, 1964, and the Indian Claims Commission is now proceeding to the determination of the net amounts due the Indians. It is anticipated that these monies will be used for improvements to their modern reservations, tribal enterprises, and scholarships.

Beginning in 1888 the missionary committee of the Women's National Indian Association became interested in the condition of the Seminoles. Four hundred acres of land west of Immokalee was purchased and a mission was established. In 1898 the Episcopal Church established the Glades Cross mission. In 1917 a state reservation of 99,200 acres was established along the southwest coast of Florida north of Shark River. The land was used by Seminoles for hunting and occasional camps were set up there but it never really served the needs of the tribe. With the establishment of the Everglades National Park in 1947 this land was included within the park boundaries. In compensation the Seminoles were given another state reserve adjacent to the Big Cypress federal reservation.

Beginning in 1888 with the appointment of the first federal Indian Agent for Florida, the federal government began to purchase land for the Seminoles. For long Immokalee was the center of federal activity and a sawmill and wood working shop were established there to train Indians in useful arts. The experiment was a dismal failure and the project was soon closed down. The Seminole reservations at present include the small Hollywood tract at Hollywood, formerly called Dania. This lies between the Florida Turnpike and U.S. Route 441 just to the west of Ft. Lauderdale in the center of much of the tourist activity in the state. It is a quite urban environment in contrast to the other more rural reservations. The Brighton Reservation northwest of Lake Okeechobee lies outside the Everglades and is somewhat higher, drier land. It is largely occupied by Muskogee speakers. The Big Cypress Reservation of 42,663 acres some distance south of Lake Okeechobee lies on the border of the Everglades and the Big Cypress Swamp and was formerly very wet. New drainage ditches have made some parts drier. Big Cypress is largely the home of Mikasukis. It is adjacent to the state reservation which is not much used. The new cross-state Everglades parkway cuts through the state reservation and will open up the area to both Indians and tourists. The Miccosukee Tribe has a separate federal reservation along the Tamiami Trail south of the state reservation and has equal access to the state reservation with the Seminole Tribe. There are scattered, mostly Mikasuki, camps along the Tamiami Trail and some Indians live within the Everglades National Park by special permits.

The State of Florida maintains a state Indian agent who is not resident on the reservation and has little actual participation in Indian affairs. He does supervise the issuing of free license plates for Seminole autos. The federal Indian agent and the headquarters of the agent are located at the Hollywood reserve, quite distant from both Brighton and Big Cypress.

SEMINOLES IN THE TWENTIETH CENTURY

The growing population of Florida failed to break the isolation of the Seminoles. Even the land boom of the 1920's disturbed them little. Their population gradually increased and they began to have sporadic jobs in the cattle industry and the growing vegetable farming as the Everglades were drained. They still, however, had no significant participation in the life of modern Florida. During World War II with the shortages of labor on cattle ranches and truck gardens in the area, Seminole women especially took jobs harvesting crops and regular cash wages began to flow into the reservations. The depression days of the 1930's had seen the development of gardens, mainly on the Brighton Reservation through the efforts of the Civilian Conservation Corps in which a number of Seminole men enlisted. The Depression years had also seen the initiation of improved herds among the Seminole which may well be the major cause of change among them.

SEMINOLE CATTLE HERDS

The Seminole, while still in northern Florida had begun to use the herds of wild cattle that resulted from the collapse of the Spanish ranches. After the Second Seminole War they had largely to abandon their cattle herding because cattle could not long survive the periods of high water. Pigs were about the only animals raised regularly by the Seminole, and these usually were semi-wild range specimens of little economic value. In the mid-thirties 500 pure bred Herefords, purchased from drought--stricken western ranges were shipped to Brighton to form the start of a tribal herd. The Hollywood (then Dania) reservation did not have enough room for cattle and Big Cypress was too wet for cattle. In 1939 the first Indian representatives were appointed as trustees of the tribal herd. In 1946 the cattle program was extended to Big Cypress where native range cattle formed the nucleus of the herd. Pure bred Brahma bulls were used to upgrade the herd and a beginning of systematic cattle raising was underway.

While pasturage and other conditions on the Brighton Reserve are poor, they are even worse at Big Cypress. Florida range cattle had developed some resistance to diseases of the tropical, humid climate and Brahma admixture proved of some advantage. More recently Angus bulls have been used to produce a better grade of beef cattle that can compete with other cattle in the Florida market. Native pasture is very poor and it takes a very large acreage to support even a single cow. Improved pasture is necessary as is the addition of minerals to the diet, drainage in the wet season, and irrigation in the dry months. To some extent the two major reservations have been able to acquire improved pasturage by leasing land for truck farms with the provision that at the end of a short lease the land be returned planted to permanent grasses. Even this scheme had not provided enough pasture and considerable expense has been undertaken to extend the acreage. The cattle experts at the Institute of Food and Agricultural Sciences at the University of Florida Experiment Station have been extremely cooperative in providing expert advice on cattle to the Seminole Agency. The lowest economically feasible herd for a family is about 50 cattle, with the desirable size at 200 head. Many of the Seminole owners of parts of the tribal herd were unwilling or unable to work herds of even the smaller size. The result has been that there has been a considerable amount of dissatisfaction with the cattle program. The Cattlemen's Association tried to enforce rules governing the size of herds, care of cattle and pasture, and all the many problems involved in modern cattle rearing. In 1966 they secured a new set of rules which gave them this power. While the result is felt by cattle experts to strengthen the operation as a whole, it has resulted in the small, marginal cattle owners being forced to sell their cows and get out of the cattle business.

Many of the problems of the Seminole tribal herd are of course unique to the south Florida environment. Others are common to cattlemen everywhere. The Indians are further confused by the fact that they feel that they must take much of the needed expert advice on faith. The meetings of the Association are conducted in English with translations, often very summary, into Mikasuki. Many Indians do not realize that their equity in their herd is gradually being increased, although they see little or no ready cash. Cattle owning seemed an ideal way to secure some income while remaining on the reservation. Most Seminole, like other Indians, do not feel able to argue with authority as represented by the agency staff. Hollywood was a long way from both Big Cypress and Brighton, and even if one knew what questions to ask, the answers were usually confusing. The program has had the beneficial result, however, of at least beginning a viable program which can make use of a large number of tribal acres. It also has had the effect of introducing at least some Seminoles to the problems of a large scale program within modern economic bounds. What has not been resolved is the question of why a small part of the tribe, the cattle owners, should benefit from the use of reservation lands while others cannot secure such benefits. In general cattle owners are the less conservative, more white-oriented members of the tribe.

THE SEMINOLES TODAY

Over the years, due in large part to the availability of at least some modern public health medicine, the Seminole population has increased very considerably from the low point of less than 300 in the late 1850's. Because so many Seminoles live off the Reservation and all move about a great deal, it is difficult to form an accurate picture of their numbers. It is clear, however, that there are about 2,000 Seminoles, including those Mikasuki living along the Tamiami Trail and in the new reservation there administered separately for the Mikasuki Tribe. A few live as far north as near Ocala where their camp forms part of the tourist attractions at Silver Springs. Especially during the 1960's change was evident in a number of aspects of Seminole life, although some social and religious aspects change very slowly. The exposure to the luxury goods of white American culture has produced many wants that must be answered by a cash economy and cannot be supplied by the old subsistence pattern.

Earning A Living

Seminole men still hunt and fish, as do most

other south Florida people in a land that still has quite abundant supplies of game. These activities, however, do not contribute any great amount of the family food, most of which is purchased in stores, often some distance from the reservation. Seminole matrons are regularly seen in the supermarkets of Okeechobee, Moore Haven, Clewiston, and Immokalee. Cash for these purchases comes from a number of sources, of which the most frequent is work in the large organized farms built on the rich drained muck of the Everglades.

Beginning in 1955 there developed a plan of renting lands on the reservations to large growers who drain, ditch, and improve it in other ways. After two years the land must be turned back to the tribe in improved pasture, generally Pangola or Bahia Pensacola grasses. There is a greater demand for improved pasture than this process can provide and the Bureau of Indian Affairs has advanced credits for the creation of more improved pasture. The leasors are all large-scale commercial companies that need large amounts of temporary labor during the winter months. Beans, tomatoes, watermelons, and many other crops are raised here which supply much of the food on northern markets. The Indians do no commercial farming for themselves, perhaps in part because of the demands that the cattle program makes on all available improved pasture. The local range-Brahma cross bred cattle on unimproved land produce only about nine pounds of beef per acre per year. At the University of Florida cattle experiment station nearby, improved breeds on proper permanent pasture have produced up to 810 pounds of better grade beef per acre per year. Seminole cattle raisers find it difficult to compete with modern farm technology. Insect pests have been a serious hazard to the cattle industry but are now slowly yielding to insecticides and the increasingly common introduced cattle egret has helped to control the noxious pests.

The Seminole people have never developed any mechanism for alloting individuals land for agricultural purposes. As the ancestral Creeks certainly had an agricultural land system based on the matrilineal clan system, it seems likely that when the Seminole were finally forced into the Everglades with very restricted amounts of tillable land, this older land-use system was abandoned. Most Seminole do have a garden plot near their chickees, but the yield is generally not enough to supply even the family's needs. Most camps raise some crops: corn, sugar cane, and sweet potatoes being the most common. The list of crops raised at least occasionally would include: pumpkins, beans, bananas, sour oranges, white lemons, custard apples, watermelons, cabbage, guavas, and mangoes. Only the older, more conservative people seem to have well tended gardens.

Wild products are still a significant element in some camps although not as important as formerly. Deer are still generally hunted. Frog legs once formed a major source of income as they brought a good price at Miami restaurants. This source, also, has declined in importance. Fish, in this land of water, are regularly taken. The tough scales of the gar fish are cleaned and sold for the manufacture of costume jewelry. Other wild sources bring in occasional cash.

The major source of money is the large farm operations, both vegetable farming and cattle ranching, located near the reservations. In the vegetable fields both men and women work in the winter harvest season, surely some of the most burdensome labor known. A few Seminole have become labor contractors who furnish a stated number of workers to the big farms. They receive a percentage of the wages from each person in return for finding the jobs and providing transportation. Most Seminoles prefer the better paying and less arduous jobs of driving trucks and tractors. While mechanization poses some threat to the more lowly forms of farm labor, recent national attention to the plight of migrant labor has resulted in some increases in pay scales and improvement in working conditions. Few Seminoles seem to support the newly emerging farm labor unions. The younger men work as cowboys on the adjacent ranches, and of course for the tribal herds. They are generally regarded as steady reliable workers and this occupation may be much more steady than the highly seasonal vegetable farm jobs. Relatively few year round jobs are available to Seminoles and the farm labor rate is too low to allow them to carry over much money into the slack season. In most cases they must depend on some other source for subsistence during at least part of the year.

For some time the manufacture of craft items has been a sporadic source of income to numerous Seminoles, both men and women. Items made for sale by men are mostly wood carvings, full sized sofkee spoons, miniature canoes, tomahawks, etc. They are generally made on a part time basis, between jobs in agriculture and there has been no development of the more creative aspects of woodcarving that have appeared on some other reservations. This lack of a well developed wood carving complex has limited the value of these items to the souvenir class and consequent rather modest prices. While some men sew, most of the famous Seminole patchwork is made by the women. Most women regularly sew for their families and Seminoles wear patchwork, at least for dress-up occasions. Nowadays many women have electric sewing machines, although a few of the older handturned kind are still in use. Patchwork jackets for men, skirts for women, and dresses for dolls make up the bulk of this sewing.

Courtesy Smithsonian Institution National Anthropological Archives

WO SEMINOLE WOMEN USING WODDEN MORTAR and pestles for pounding corn, for ›ng a major item of Seminole diet. These women were photographed by Charles arney Cory, Sr. about 1890. The dresses are typical of the period with voluminous :irts having a short flounce below the knees. Most Seminole women wore very umerous strings of beads around the neck over short capes. Beads and cloth were ıajor items of trade with the local trading posts.

Recently some innovations have been appearing such as drawstring purses, some with basketry bases, and applique patchwork strips for sewing to sportshirts. Small dolls made of palmetto fiber with patchwork dresses are a popular item with tourists as they are cheap, readily portable, and appealing to the young. The tribal Arts and Crafts Center at Hollywood has offered a steady market for these productions as have the innumerable souvenir stands throughout south Florida. The rise in tourism and especially the increase in summer tourists have made craft work a more significant contribution to Seminole life. There is not, however, any intensive development of crafts as a full-time occupation and the consequent development of outstanding artists in these fields. While the Seminoles make and use some basketry, it seems not to be a significant element of craft sales as it has become on many reservations. Pottery is apparently not made anymore and its production would be difficult to recreate. In spite of the heavy tourism of south Florida, craft production does not seem to offer many rewards as a way of life, in spite of the fact that the colorful patchwork is uniquely Seminole and has a wide inherent appeal.

Various State and Federal sources of funds are available to the Seminole. A very limited number, less than 3% of the Seminoles, are recipients of state-federal welfare. About an equal number receive social security payments. A few men are employed by the Bureau of Indian Affairs in road work and land operations, or by state or county agencies. In general the salaries of these men are above minimum subsistence standards, but some 60% of the families have incomes below $3,000 per year. It is clear that Seminoles are underemployed and poorly paid. The programs of the Office of Economic Opportunity have been of more benefit to the Indians on the reservations than any other single source of federal or state support. There are several Headstart Schools, which employ young women as fulltime teach aides. A nursery school employs mothers and also provides a much-needed day care program for working mothers. More women are employed in the kitchen which serves hot lunches. The Community Action Program of O.E.O. provided the position of social worker's aide which, it was hoped, would be filled by an Indian. Both men and women have tried to keep this job but conflicts with other Indians, with the white hierarchy, have forced most incumbents to resign. The basic problem is that Seminoles do not like to "boss" other Indians and do not like to express strong opinions to the white administrative personnel. The result has been that the position of aide is only gradually developing into the much needed channel of communication. The Neighborhood Youth Program was the first opportunity for juveniles to have a steady income. As it operates mostly in the summer school vacation period it has been very effective. Again there have been a number of conflicts which have rested on the inability of Indians adequately to communicate with the white administration.

Some Indians from both Big Cypress and Brighton have found jobs at the electronic components plant established in Hollywood by the Industrial Development Program of the Bureau of Indian Affairs. English is a necessary skill for work in the plant and thus many of the more conservative, older people are barred. Taking a job in the plant means, for Brighton and Big Cypress residents, moving to Hollywood where land is very scarce and the urban atmosphere repells many Indians from the distant reservations. While nearly a hundred Indians have worked at the plant since it was opened, many have been replaced by non-Indians who were more adjusted to the regimen of regular hours required in factory operations. An agency-sponsored wood working shop on Big Cypress failed because of these problems. While some Seminoles can adjust to the long hours and regular work schedules demanded by industry, the learning of the necessary attitudes is slow for most of them. Perhaps the mild climate with an abundance of game available reduces the impulse to accommodate to the white man's ways.

Political Organization

Today the formal organization of the Bureau of Indian Affairs dominates the political organization of the Seminole. They possess a dual organization under the provisions of the Wheeler-Howard Act of 1934 which provided for establishment of formal, legal, tribal governing bodies. The Seminoles ratified a constitution in 1957 which formally established the Seminole Tribe of Florida. Somewhat later those Mikasuki living along the Tamiami Trail formally organized as the Miccosukee Tribe which has a separate administration and reservation. Many Mikasuki speakers, however, are members of The Seminole Tribe of Florida and the division is mainly between those who live along the Trail and those Mikasuki living on the Big Cypress Reservation. The Mikasuki Tribe is much more independent of white control than the Seminole Tribe of Florida, maintaining the historical antagonism to white affairs that has been so characteristic of the Florida Seminoles as a whole.

Membership in the Seminole Tribe of Florida is restricted to those persons of Seminole blood and must be applied for. The constitution and by-laws provide that one-quarter of Seminole Indian blood is necessary for eligibility. Approval of an application for membership by a majority of the members of the tribal council is necessary. Approximately two-thirds of the residents of the three reservations are enrolled members of the tribe. Other members live off-reservation in Miami, Ft. Pierce, Immokalee, and especially along the Tamiami Trail. This constitution was ratified by a great majority of those voting, some 55% of all the Indians eligible. The Tribe has jurisdiction, under the Bureau of Indian Affairs, of the three Federal reservations of Hollywood, Brighton, and Big Cypress. The State reservation is administered jointly by The Seminole Tribe of Florida and the Miccosukee Tribe, which solely administers the Tamiami Trail reserve. The constitution gives the Indians the right to govern themselves in certain spheres specified by the Bureau of Indian Affairs.

The five members of the tribal council are elected by secret ballot and majority vote. The chairman of this council is elected at-large, with three members elected from the tribal reservations. The fifth member is the president of the board of directors of the Seminole Tribe of Florida, Inc., which will be described below. Committee members are elected for a term of two years and there are selected committees and a secretary-treasurer to the council. Council membership is open to any person over twenty-one years of age, a member of the Tribe, and a resident for the previous four years of the reservation from which he will be elected.

Candidates must in addition to these qualifications present a petition of ten voters of their reservation. The tribal council can deal with federal, state, and local governments, employ legal counsel, manage tribal lands, pass certain ordinances, and generally conduct the political activity of the tribe. The council passed a resolution giving the state and pertinent counties both civil and criminal jurisdiction over the three reservations. This was ratified by the Florida Legislature in 1961 but has not resulted in any major extension of state or county authority over the reservations. Most Indians feel that any Seminole who calls in county officers is acting against the best interests of the tribe and state laws are usually enforced on the reservations only when they involve white persons.

Organized at the same time as the Seminole Tribe of Florida, the Seminole Tribe of Florida, Inc. is the business organization of the tribe. It is a federally chartered corporation governed by a board of five directors. This separation of power is usual among Indian tribes who have organized under the Wheeler-Howard Act. Charged with the development and management of tribal resources it is potentially a very powerful body. The president of the board of directors is elected at-large, three are elected from the three reservations, and the fifth is the vice-president who is also the chairman of the tribal council. There is thus an interlocking of the directorate of the two tribal entities.

All members of the Seminole Tribe of Florida are also shareholders in the Seminole Tribe of Florida, Inc. Meetings of the shareholders may be called by a petition or by the board of directors, but there have been only two such meetings since the corporation was organized in 1957. Most actions of the corporations have resulted from decisions of the board of directors. Their authority is limited by the need for authorization from the Bureau of Indian Affairs, and ultimately from the Secretary of the Interior in regard to land sales or sales of mineral rights. The corporation can, however, borrow funds and lend funds to shareholders from the Indian credit fund established by the Bureau for tribes which have incorporated under the Reorganization Act.

Accomplishments of the corporation are the administration of certain escrow funds accruing to the tribe through such things as rights of way across reservation lands. They have also formed the Seminole Indian Land Development Enterprise which oversees the development of improved pasture at Big Cypress and Brighton reservations. Funds for this work come from leases, from grazing fees paid by Indians who own cattle, and from certain federal funds available to the agency. The corporation also makes low interest loans to eligible members for houses, cattle, and small businesses. In addition it has created the Seminole Okalee Indian Village and the Seminole Arts and Crafts Center, both located at Hollywood. As Hollywood, though so far from the major reservation lands, is in the midst of the south Florida Gold Coast tourist area, these enterprises have proved highly popular.

The charter of the corporation specifies that the Bureau of Indian Affairs has ultimate approval of the fiscal activities of the corporation. This has meant that Indians who borrow money for cattle, houses, or businesses are subject to a great deal of control by the bureaucratic hierarchy. The council may employ lawyers to represent tribal interests but the choice of the attorney and his fee is subject to approval by the Bureau. An agency representative attends all meetings and is usually the only person present who knows the rules of formal procedure, the applicable statutes, etc. Few Indians have any knowledge of business or legal matters, few can write, and they are generally quite confused by formal procedures. The control of the Bureau of Indian Affairs is pervasive, often subtle, and while it generates frequent resentment from the Indians, they are very unsure about how to counter it.

The ancestral Creek political system, closely related to the religious system, consisted of town chiefs of two sorts. Peace chiefs were at least

GROUP OF SEMINOLE MEN, WOMEN, and children around a cooking fire at a commercial camp, 1921. The patchwork shown here is largely composed of horizonta
bands, with very few more complex designs. The man wears the older style of "big
Shirt" that seems to have descended from very early Seminole clothing patterns. The

Courtesy Smithsonian Institution National Anthropological Archives

ommercial camps served as tourist attractions for many years in the Miami area and ontinue until the present along the Tamiami Trail and at the Seminole Hollywood eservation.

partly hereditary in specified clans and served also as religious leaders in the great tribal ceremonies. The elaborate hierarchy of these chiefs testifies to a complex political system. War leaders were very largely selected on the basis of demonstrated ability, not only in warfare but in oratory and leadership as well. A man endowed with enough charisma could win to a position of eminence among the war chiefs even though his mother's clan was not one with the hereditary right to nominate peace chiefs. In addition there was a council for each town composed of respected elders. This political system was closely interwoven with the religious system and remnants of much of the organization survived the transition to Florida. The great reduction in numbers as a result of the Seminole Wars made such a system inoperative. There simply were not enough people to run the system and there was little need for such a governing body in the small camps of the 19th century. Remnants of the older pattern did, however, continue in the Court Day of the Green Corn Festival where crimes against individuals or the group were judged and punishments assigned. This system has now almost totally disappeared to be replaced by the paternalistic forms of the Seminole Tribe of Florida and the Seminole Tribe of Florida, Inc. There is little incentive toward positions of responsibility and many persons shun the inevitable exercise of authority that such positions bring. Seminole of both sexes are reluctant to advance their own ideas at the expense of others. Thus, there is little incentive or mechanism to select for potential leaders. Only in rare cases of conflict with outsiders will Indians assert their rights. The ideal is to discuss any potential action until a general consensus is reached and all opposition is silent. This is not very effective in business dealings with the outside world and the Indians suffer from this limitation. The blood which produced such leaders as Emporer Brim, Alexander, McGillivray, the Prophet Francis, Micanopy, and Osceola now avoids leadership as a threat to the exercise of peaceful relations between individuals. Because of small scattered camps, low population, and isolation the Seminoles were forced by circumstance to drop their former effective methods of selecting leaders. As the Nation emerges into the main stream of the 20th century there is once more the population size and need for vigorous leadership.

The Seminole Camp

The basic residential, social, and economic unit among the Seminoles is the camp, both a physical location and a closely related unit of people. Physically the camp is a site, usually rather charming, from which brush and small trees have been cleared. Placed on higher ground it is, nevertheless, often surrounded by water, swamp, or the sawgrass plains. Today camps are rather permanent, often with a drilled well, although formerly there were a good many quite temporary hunting or frogging camps. Each basic family making up the camp has its own chickee, the typical Seminole house so well adapted to the hot, rainy climate and the technology available to the Indians. The chickee is a simple framework of upright logs firmly planted in the ground to support a peaked roof covered with palmetto thatch. While sawn boards were preferred for the roof framework, on occasion small poles were used. Floors are always raised for the sleeping houses, but not for the cookhouse. These floors, raised about 18 inches above the ground and constructed of either sawn boards or split logs are used for sleeping, lounging, and a place for the women to sew.

Small in size, averaging 8 by 15 feet, and made of mostly local materials, the Seminole house could be made by one man in five or six days of part time work. If the house itself is simple, the equipment is scanty. A mosquito net of muslin is a necessity in the swampy land. A few clothes and other possessions are hung from the rafters. The older pattern was that the hand-operated sewing machine was about the only item of equipment in most houses. The open sides and ends provide for maximum use of what breezes may be available and do not offer any resistance to the hurricanes that devastate the region from time to time. Fleeing to the few spots of high ground at the first subtle warnings of a hurricane, the Seminoles could return when the floods that accompany these storms had subsided and find their chickees virtually intact. Perhaps the palmetto fronds of the roof would need replacement, but this was no major task. By experiment and patient trial the Seminole, when they moved into the Everglades, learned to build the best house that they were able for the conditions of their new environment.

In the center of the encircling individual family houses is the cookhouse, highly similar to the sleeping chickees but for lacking a floor. Here all the cooking for the entire camp takes place over a central fire of radiating logs. Usually one or more tables were located at the ends of the cookhouse, not for eating but for preparing food. The women took the cooked food to an eating chickee at one side of the camp. Any member of the camp, and most visitors, was welcome to help himself to whatever food was prepared. Usually this included *sofkee* the traditional drink and food of most southern Indians. Prepared from hominy, roughly crushed corn that has been soaked in wood ash lye, it was cooked with water to form a thin, slightly tart gruel. It was usually to be found near the fire in a large pot from which it was dipped with a long slightly angled wooden ladle, the "Sofkee spoons" still made as sales items for the tourist trade. Now most women buy commercially prepared corn grits at local stores but a liking for *sofkee* persists among the Seminole, as it does among most southern Indian tribes. At the cookhouse is stored most of the kitchen equipment of the camp.

Formerly the camp had a "baby house" at the edge of the camp. A woman retired to have her child in a small shelter some distance from the camp. Remaining there for four days, she then returned to the "baby house" at the edge of the camp where she was to remain with her child for four months. During this whole period she cooked her own food and men avoided touching her, lest they fall ill. Today most Seminole women have babies in the hospital at Clewiston under contracts negotiated by the Agency. The four months of isolation has almost completely disappeared, although some women still stay there about a month.

Within this physical setting live the members of the camp, a group of individuals all related to the central woman in the camp. While the camp is usually named for some man, often the husband of the oldest woman, it actually is organized around this woman. A camp thus consists of a woman, her daughters, their husbands, unmarried sons, children of the women, and even grandchildren. Some camps

Photograph by William D. Boehmer

ᴍRS. STELLA SMITH USING A LONG-HANDLED LADLE to stir cane syrup cooking in a huge iron syrup-kettle at Billie Bowlegs' camp. This camp raised its own patch of cane to produce the sweetening.

consist of only a single person, often an old man. Others consist of a single basic family, mother, father, and children, with sometimes a few extra kinfolk. The older form of camp was most commonly the extended matrilineal family described above. Consisting of from seven to perhaps sixteen persons, the average was probably about ten persons. When a woman marries, she brings her husband back to her mother's camp where her kin help him build the family chickee. Seminole marriages are rather fragile. If a couple does not get along, the husband will simply leave and return to his mother's camp. He does help support his wife and children, but in the eyes of the Seminoles this is primarily the responsibility of the mother and her kin. The mother's brother, in particular, has the responsibility for seeing that his sisters, mother, and all family children are properly provided for in the Seminole system.

This maternal camp certainly reflects an older Creek and Seminole traditional organization of the family around the woman. Even today women seem to feel more responsibility for their children than do men. The old clan rules governing marriage are still practiced to some extent and the clan system still controls some aspects of a person's behavior. Membership in a clan descended through the female line, that is a person belonged to the clan of his or her mother. Marriage between clan members was forbidden, meaning that all the husbands in a camp belonged to different clans than their wives and children. Among the Muskogee of Brighton Reservation there are five clans with the totemic names: Panther (usually called Tiger), Bird, Talahasee (Old Town), Deer, and Snake. On the Big Cypress Reservation there are nine clans named: Wind, Tiger, Otter, Bird, Deer, Snake, Bear, Talwathlako (Big Town), and Wolf. The names of the clans are mainly, now at least, a means of identifying a clan by giving it a name. Each clan had an origin legend in which a supernatural ancestor was Bird, Tiger, Snake, etc. The two non-totemic clans, Talahasee (Old Town) among the Muskogee and a relatively recent Talwathlako (Big Town) are exceptions to the rule that the clans have animal names, and are difficult to explain. It is said that the Talwathlako clan was created recently to make a place for non-Indian women who married Seminoles and moved into the camps. Talahasee, meaning Old Town is a revered name among the Creeks and Seminoles, occurring in the forms of Talwa-assee, Tallahassee, and Tulsa. Perhaps in the past Seminole considered a town as much of a being as an animal such as deer or panther.

At least on the Brighton Reservation the clans are linked into pairs or trios. The Panther-Deer linkage is strong and clan members should not marry a member of the linked clan. The linkage of Bird and Talahasee is equally strong with

Snake being somewhat more weakly linked to Bird. These linkings produce a weak dual division within the tribe with Panther-Deer standing in contrast to Bird-Talahasee-Snake. This seems to be a remnant of formerly important dual divisions among the Seminole and other southern tribes. Aside from control of marriage the clans have little function today and in the greatly reduced population there seems to be little purpose to clan organization. Formerly clans were a necessary means of identifying kinsmen in a much larger population and clans were important in many political and religious contexts. Today most Seminole can readily identify their clan and many feel a vague pride that their clan is in some way better than others.

In recent years chickees are disappearing as a result of being replaced by concrete block houses, built with loans from the corporation. It often proves difficult to move an extended matrilineal family into a house of the newer type. Where each basic family formerly had its own family chickee, they now must put up with only one rather crowded room. The move into more modern houses is accompanied by an increase in appliances, electric sewing machines, refrigerators, stoves, television sets, etc. as well as by a higher proportion of families which are separate from the older extended family system. As the Seminole become more and more involved in wage labor and more attracted to the consumer goods of modern life, the old family structure must adapt to the changed conditions and expectations.

Although fragile with frequent divorce the Seminole family remains a powerful force in shaping the lives of its members. The dominant position of the women means that they exercise more authority than do the men in most decisions. Marriage is only rarely performed in the reservation churches or by the local county authorities. Young Seminole simply set up housekeeping and are recognized by the camp as being married. The state recognizes these unions as binding common law marriages. Divorce is easy, with the man leaving the camp of his wife's group. Babies of both sexes are wanted and are loved intensely, especially when very young. Parents and kin pet and handle them almost constantly. After a baby begins to walk he is usually turned over to older sisters who continue almost as indulgent care as he enjoyed earlier. As the child grows older this love and affection give way to increasing indifference. The child is simply ignored and there are simply no means of interaction between juveniles and adults.

Seminole parents still love their older children and often express pride in their accomplishments. What they lack is any pattern of training and educating the older children. In the old days two patterns of training in adult ways were present, both now very largely absent.

Story telling by grandmothers was a definite educational device. The stories, often strongly mixed with white elements, always told the way things should be done. The constant repetition of the right way of behavior and the results of asocial action were a strong element in producing socially acceptable behavior. The breakup of the older family system has left a void in the education of children. Parents also used to have the device of scratching as a disciplinary device. This was done as a punishment and especially at the great annual Green Corn Festival in the late spring. The children who had misbehaved were scratched with the needle sharp teeth in a gar fish jaw or by needles set in a wooden holder. Scratching was also regarded as part of boys assuming fully adult status. With the decline of the old religious patterns and conversion to Christianity, scratching has virtually disappeared. Seminole children are never spanked, or even disciplined in any way. Even more serious is the fact that children and parents seem to have absolutely no communication. Especially in the urban setting of Hollywood this has had serious consequences in a marked rise in juvenile deliquency. Gasoline sniffing, vandalism, teenage drinking, and more serious behavior problems have greatly increased. Children respect their parents but throughout childhood there is an increasing pattern of indifference and distance.

The strongest bonds are between girls and their mother's sister who is always ready with advice and help. Even this relationship does not result in much communication, however. There is no system of authority so that the Seminole child grows up with the behavior pattern of being able to ask or offer advice, but no one has the right to command. The result is that the Seminole grows into an adult who may talk with another of his same age about problems, but there is literally no mechanism of communication and authority.

Perhaps the most distinctive and widely recognized thing about the Florida Seminole is their colorful dress, worn at least on occasion by women, men and children. Commonly called patchwork it is a brightly colored, intricate style manufactured by the women, formerly on hand turned sewing machines, while they now greatly prefer more modern electric ones. It is not an ancient form of dress but something uniquely Seminole, constantly changing as the women develop new styles. The basic dress of the women is a long skirt, reaching nearly to the ground and quite full. Over the bodice they often wear a cape over the shoulders, extending to the waist, usually of a solid color and often of thin, transparent cloth. Small girl babies are usually dressed in a tiny version of this basic, horizontally banded dress. Some especially prized skirts have more than forty horizontal bands, each composed of many different elements. The older women still wear a great number of bead strings around the neck, often covering the area from shoulders to chin, sometimes weighing as much as 25 pounds. Younger women now seem often to prefer a triangular scarf, tied at the back. Older women sometimes still wear the traditional elaborate hair arrangement that is rapidly disappearing among young people. To prepare this elaborate head dress the long hair is combed forward over the face. Then a large disc is tied around the head with most of its expanse extending toward the front. The hair is then pulled back over the frame and fastened at the back. The whole is usually covered with a hairnet. The result is a helmet-shaped creation that has a brim-like extension over the forehead.

Today the usual dress of men is work clothes, commonly blue jeans. The older styles persist, however, for special occasions and some men still wear the long and short shirts of sixty years ago. The long shirt, sometimes called a medicine dress, is a long-sleeved dress reaching to below the knee. The short, and more popular, shirt, also with long sleeves, reaches to the waist. Both are composed of many horizontal bands of patchwork. At some times zig-zag rickrack, purchased in stores is interspersed with the patchwork bands. The most common material for both men's and women's dress is brightly

Photograph by John I. Griffin

RS. MARY MOTLOW OSCEOLA, mother of long-time Florida Seminole Tribal Chair-
an William Osceola. In her late 80's, Mrs. Osceola dresses up with pounds of bead
ecklaces above her bright blouse and skirt. Her hair is done in traditional style to
shion a "brim" over her forehead.

colored cotton, although silk, rayon, and modern synthetics appear in more elaborate versions reserved for ceremonial occasions. Men, women, and children often go barefoot, perhaps an advantage in the wet lands of the Everglades. Young men, even before the current modes of dress, often wore their hair quite long and combed back from the forehead. Older men sometimes shaved the head back of the ears, but this is no longer seen.

Seminole patchwork is not an ancestral form, although the style of the long men's dress does go back to late colonial times. As a style, patchwork developed among the Seminole only after the introduction of the first hand-turned sewing machines in 1905. Patchwork is a living craft in which both Seminole women and men take great pride. The informed student of Seminole costume can assign approximate dates to the varying styles of the patchwork bands, the amount of rickrack, and other details. As a living, changing art, it is one of the best expressions of the uniqueness of the Seminoles.

To make a patchwork band that will be combined into a skirt or shirt, the Seminole seamstress first takes three to as many as seven strips of cloth from one-half to perhaps two inches wide which are sewn together along their long sides. This produces a band of parallel stripes of colors. She then cuts the band, either at right angles or diagonally, into narrow

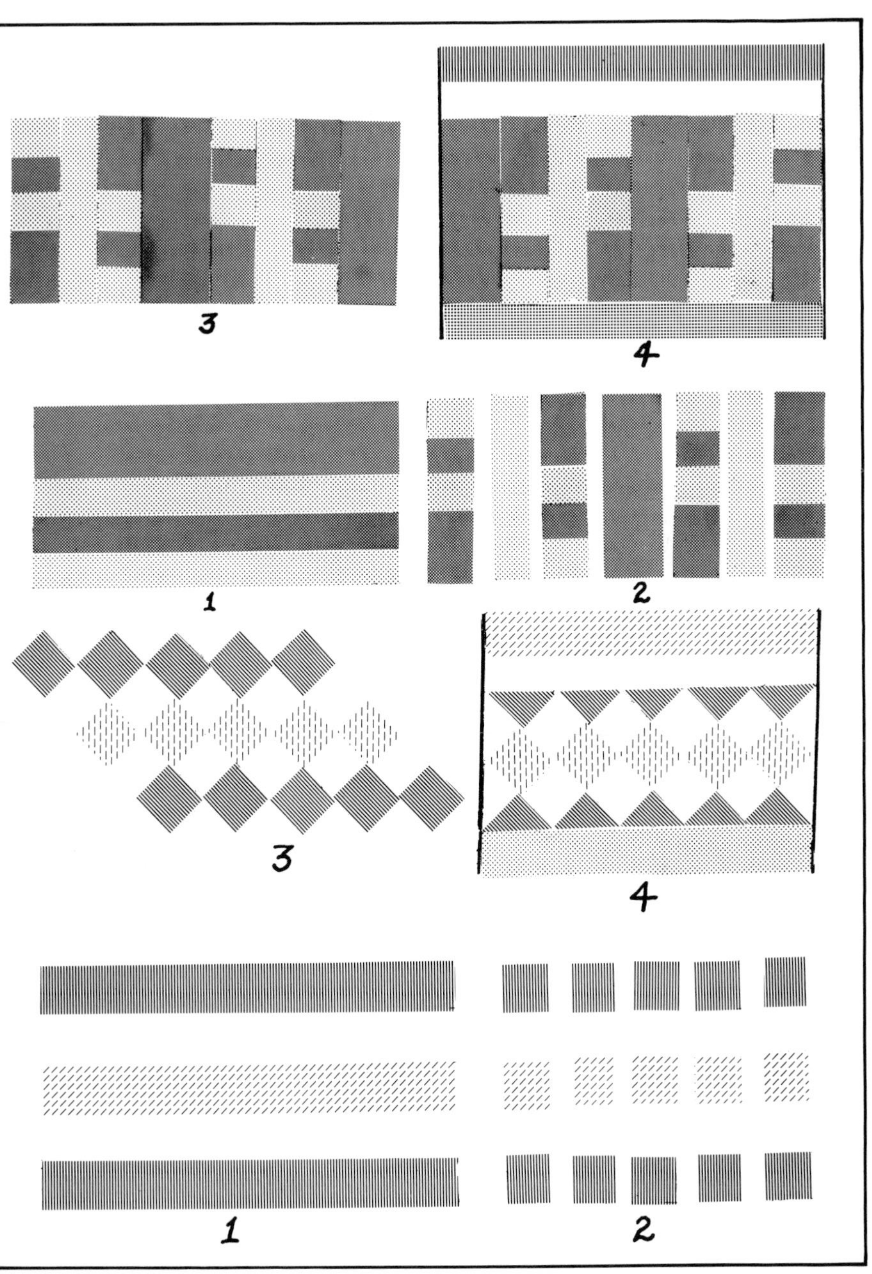

ATCH WORK DIAGRAM

segments, each composed of contrasting blocks of colors. These segments are then rearranged and resewn into a new band, the original stripes now forming bands often with highly intricate designs that seem to be composed of tiny squares and rectangles of contrasting color. The composite bands are then sewn to bands of solid colors, sometimes figured material, or of contrasting materials to form the basic fabric of the garment. Rickrack or braid may be applied to the garment in varying numbers of bands. The basic design is always of contrasting bands of color. The result sounds horrible, but is a magnificent example of a highly developed craft.

About fifty years ago many men wore a sort of turban of brightly colored cloth, wrapped around a framework of bark. This was decorated with two or three upstanding plumes and recalls the early turbans worn by Osceola, Neamathla, and other leaders during the Second Seminole War. Now most of the younger men favor western style ten-gallon hats, often decorated patchwork, beadwork, leather, or rarely silver bands. Except for the multiple strings of beads worn by the women, Seminole costume does not include much beadwork so characteristic of many tribes. Formerly the Seminole fashioned small circular silver discs to be fastened on the clothing, especially of women. In recent years this craft became nearly extinct but is now being revived by one or two craftsmen. Whereas

Photograph by William D. Boehmer

RS. EMMA MICCO repairing a maize sifting basket for her own household use on the righton Reservation a few years after the second World War.

formerly these silver discs were hammered from silver coins, now commercial silver is purchased from craft supply shops.

Except for patchwork, the Seminole seem to have weakly developed crafts. Wooden sofkee spoons are made, used commonly, and sold to tourists. Some basketry is made in typical southeastern Indian style. This is a shallow basket with rounded but square cornered base. The principal use is as a sifter for use in making hominy, in which case it has an open mesh bottom. A few other baskets are made for use around the home and some are made for sale. Palmetto fiber is the common material, not one of the best for sturdy, lasting baskets. Most are undecorated and are not of forms and appearance that make them widely useable in the white society. Large wooden mortars and pestles for corn grinding are hollowed out of large logs and formerly graceful canoes were regularly made for use in crossing the shallow grassy plains of the Everglades. Many of the tools and equipment of daily life, once made by the Indians, are now purchased in the nearby towns. Except for patchwork clothing, the articles that the Seminoles make are for sale to the tourists and do not seem to be part of a vigorous craft tradition.

Seminole Religion

Today the majority of Seminoles are

Christian, mostly of the Baptist or Methodist groups. Missionaries had been active for over a century without making more than a handful of converts until the period of World War II. At that time several Oklahoma Baptist missionaries were active in the area and one of the most famous medicine men was converted. Since then the old pagan religion has virtually disappeared. While the Episcopal church maintained a mission station at Immokalee for many years, few if any converts were made. Recently the Church of Jesus Christ of Latter Day Saints has been active in the area and the Linguistic Institute has been working on the translation of the Gospels into Mikasuki. Native missionaries from Oklahoma are more effective, however, to judge by the number of converts.

Small frame churches are found on each of the reservations where missionaries from Hollywood sporadically hold services. More frequent are services conducted by reservation deacons. At these services the hymns, sermons, and announcements are all in the native languages, Muskogee for Brighton, Mikasuki for the Big Cypress. Monthly Sunday night suppers are well attended by the older members and there is a Women's Missionary Society. A Bible school was operated during the summer until its time was shifted in order not to conflict with the Headstart and nursery programs operated by O.E.O. The churches serve as the principal way in which people hear of important announcements as the services constitute the largest regular public gatherings. While announcements of all kinds are made from the pulpits, the deacons rarely preach about contemporary problems. The major message is personal salvation and redemption. Most Christian converts profess to have nothing to do with the old religion.

The old religion, closely tied to the political organization, involved a number of elements complexly interrelated. There was a major diety, Hisigita-imisi in Muskogee, the Master of breath who controlled life, the universe, and man. Animals, birds, and plants all possessed spirits who could affect men for good and evil. A series of great ceremonies was held throughout the year, of which the last to disappear have been the Green Corn Dance in late June or early July, and the Hunting Dance in the fall. These were primarily run by and for the men, with women excluded from the more important parts.

The Green Corn Dance lasted eight, or more recently, four days. More or less social dances alternated with ritual dances purified the square ground, and prepared the town for the start of the new year. The basic symbolism of the Green Corn Dance was that it celebrated the ripening to milk stage of the new corn crop and served to usher in a new annual cycle. On Court Day all sins against individuals or the group were judged and punished. Boys were ceremonially scratched to strengthen them, and magical teas were drunk to purify and strengthen the participants. The tribal medicine bundle was brought out by the medicineman, carefully opened, each item inspected. At dawn of the final day, after a final inspection of the medicine objects in the bundle the medicineman takes it back to the east, now fortified by the songs, the medicines, the rituals. The medicine holds all those powerful things of nature and the universe that can be mobilized for the sake of the Seminoles. Only by the proper performance of the Green Corn Dance can the forces of good that come from the Master of Breath be made available to the Indians. The Green Corn Dance was primarily a ceremony of each major town and every man had to return to his natal village, and sit with his mother's clan for this feast or incur severe penalties. With the reduction in Seminole population and the breakup of towns into small camps, the great festival became difficult to perform. Probably, however, it is only within the last generation that it has been virtually abandoned. Now an annual rodeo and a different pow-wow serve as great get togethers for people in the widely scattered camps.

Besides serving as director of the Green Corn Dance, the medicineman can use his magical skill to cure a wide range of ills. He must have a natural aptitude for this position and then must engage in a long and arduous apprenticeship to an older medicineman. While his treatment generally involves giving an herbal tea, he must also know the proper magical prayer to accompany the tea. To learn the symptoms of various diseases, what plants, or combinations of plants are indicated, how each plant is to be gathered, what parts to use, and how to prepare the teas involves tremendous memory for a host of detail. The magical formulas or songs must be repeated exactly during both the preparation and the administration in order to be effective. Even when modern medicine became available many of the Seminoles still called for the services of the medicineman. Both the medicineman and his patients understood that his cures were achieved as much by magical power as by the innate qualities of the plants he used. Thus, the more successful a healer might be, the more apt he might be to be charged with sorcery, the use of magic to injure as well as cure. Some of the famous recent medicinemen among the Seminoles became converts to Christianity after the Second World War and now will have nothing to do with magical curing. While their major function was to cure illness and direct the annual ceremony, they also were keepers of the tribal medicine bundle and were believed to control the weather by bringing or holding off storms. In general medicinemen were respected according to their success as healers,

Courtesy Smithsonian Institution National Anthropological Archives

HE DISPERSION OF THE SEMINOLES into small camps brought them into very ıtimate association with nature, as shown by their taming of wild animals such as ıe orphaned deer shown in this photograph of Billy Bowlegs in 1892. There have een a long line of Seminole men bearing the famous name of the leader of the 'hird Seminole War. His turban has a silver band and he wears silver earrings, all ammered from silver coins. His finger woven sash has designs woven in white beads. 'he use of multiple neckerchiefs was common at the time.

although they might also be feared as potential sorcerers. Medicinemen are paid in kind, cloth, pigs, etc. but probably never fully supported themselves by this means, usually having other sources of family support.

Today, while most Seminoles go regularly to the public clinic and to the hospital in Clewiston, they also still consult medicinemen for many ills. The native healers offer help for troubling dreams, unrequited love, and similar problems which the modern clinic does not attempt to treat. At present there is at least one medicinewoman among the Big Cypress people, but it is not clear how common this may be. Medicine men and women attend the clinic and make use of modern techniques as enthusiastically as do the rest of the tribe.

Reservation Health

A clinic operates at least two days each week supported by U.S. Public Health, Agency, State, and County funds. In addition doctors under contract to the Bureau of Indian Affairs visit the reservations two days each month. Hospitals in the area have contracts with the Agency to provide services for serious or emergency problems, including child birth. Today most babies are born in local hospitals. The clinic provides routine immunization shots for children, as well as for older persons. Many men need and get regular tetanus boosters. Much of the clinic activity revolves around the preventive shots for children so that child and infant mortality has fallen greatly in recent years. The clinics provide birth control pills as the health of many women has been seriously threatened by closely spaced births. It is probable that the health clinics on the reservations and the contractual services available are the major cause of the sharp rise in Seminole population in recent years.

Hookworm is endemic on the reservations with the young and old suffering most severely. The Seminoles are probably the only major group today which is infected severely with this infestation. Lack of sanitation in the old-style camps and the practice of most Seminole of going barefoot are the major causes. Animal hookworms, from dogs and cats, produce other less serious symptoms but an extremely painful irritation under the skin which is quite difficult to cure. The clinic personnel have conducted a campaign for wearing of shoes, but this has often meant that Indians wear them when they visit the clinic or go into town, occasions when the danger of infection is considerably less than in the camps. The clinic treats the resulting severe anemia and tries to encourage practices which will reduce the likelihood of reinfection.

Due to the hot, humid climate, lack of sanitary facilities, and general pattern of life diarrhea is common among the Indians. Epidemics of mumps, hepatitis, and other contagious infections are apt to strike the reservation at any time. About three per cent of the population is diabetic, for which the clinic provides insulin shots.

The Seminoles are remarkably clean, bathing daily and washing their hair frequently. Clothing is also kept clean in spite of rather primitive laundry facilities in the past. Seminole men are often stocky, partly as a result of vigorous outdoor work patterns. Women, on the other hand, are often greatly overweight, as much as 75 pounds. This is largely caused by excessive eating, except for the diabetics who often are especially obese. The diet is generally good, containing an abundance of fruits and meats with most meals. It is, however, rich in starches and carbonated drinks are very popular. Habits of over-eating are reinforced by a cultural preference for large, heavy women.

Few Indians wear glasses, and only very old persons have hearing difficulties. Dental caries are common, the result of the poor care and an abundance of sweets and sweet drinks. The prenatal and early postnatal care for both mothers and children has reduced infant mortality to about that of the general population. Most health authorities agree that, compared to other low income reservation populations, the Seminole present a picture of unusually fine physical condition.

Two major problems do occur on the reservations: alcoholism and gasoline sniffing. Alcoholism is more prevalent among older persons although some juveniles, especially at Hollywood, have begun drinking. It is probable that misuse of alcohol is no more serious than in the general population of comparable economic and educational status. Gasoline sniffing, however, is a much more serious problem as it produces irreversible changes in the brain which incapacitate the individual. It seems to have begun after World War II as a revolt against the stagnation and boredom of the reservation. Today there are a few young adults who became addicts and are now almost totally unaware of the world around them and unable to provide for themselves in any way. The practice seems not to be spreading, perhaps because of the obvious detrimental results.

Education

In the old days education was in the home, learning by doing reinforced by the myths and legends which repeated the basic value system of the Indian way of life. Girls learned the tasks of adult homemakers from observation and participation with their mothers and grandmothers in the matrilineal extended family. Boys learned hunting and farming skills from their fathers or maternal uncles. All this was reinforced by the myths and tales, told often by the grandmothers within the intimate family circle. Now Seminole children are subject to the state truancy law and must attend school until the age of sixteen. The knowledge of the old way has less value than formerly and the formal education system interferes with the learning of the older skills practiced by adults. There has developed a serious generation gap between adults and young, along with a lack of fit between the education that the child receives and both his home life and his expectations of adult activities.

There are federally supported day schools on the reservations which teach the children through the fourth grade. These are supplemented by Headstart programs which attempt to prepare the young for formal schooling. In few if any Indian homes is English the first language. Even with the Headstart program, many children must spend the first grade learning enough English to allow them to begin the first grade again the next year. Teachers in the Headstart program and the day school have Indian assistants, but still the break to an English program is a major one. Starting with the fifth grade, the children go to the county schools by bus. Big Cypress children go to Clewiston, while Brighton children go to Moore Haven. The long bus rides, one hour for Big Cypress each way, mean that the student is not able to participate in any extra-curricular activities. Headstart and special summer programs attempt to bridge the gap to the English-speaking world, but many children must still spend an extra year in the first grade to acquire enough skills in the language to begin their formal education. Those achievement tests which do not depend on a command of English strongly suggest that the Seminole children are fully the equal of the general population, but they continue to suffer language deficiencies and the lack of home situations that encourage study and reading. For the children of Big Cypress the ninety-mile, two-hour bus ride is a very severe restriction on both free time and study time. The schools of Collier County at Immokalee are closer and might be more fitted for Indian children as Immokalee is a large shipping point for truck produce with a consequent population of other minority children in its schools. Many children express a preference for the schools in Immokalee. The Bureau of Indian Affairs, however, chose to send them to Clewiston, largely because the Big Cypress Reservation is located in Hendry County. The Indian bureau sees attending public schools as a step toward assimilation into the general population. They seem not to recognize that attendance at off-reservation schools is a major source for the generation gap and for the loss of Indianness in the current school-age groups.

Few Seminoles have finished high school as the incentives to get a certificate seem not to be especially strong. Jobs in the vegetable fields are available, but few better ones are to be found in the reservation areas. The lack of any real communication between parents and children in the rapidly changing times means that while parents may approve of more education, they fail to convey their concern to the child. Few Seminole homes have any books and there is no secluded place to study. Indian boarding schools at the high school level are far away and are regarded as places for exceptionally unruly students. More girls than boys finish high school, perhaps because they see the chance for secretarial jobs in the area. Tribal leaders have encouraged young people to finish high school and attend college, for which some scholarships are available. They, however, fail to make a determined campaign for more education due to the pattern of being reluctant to interfere with another person's affairs.

While some Seminoles with more than the tribal average of education have sought, and often held, elective offices in the tribe or the corporation, education in itself is not a road to leadership within the tribe. The Seminole believe strongly that group decisions, whether for a family camp or the entire tribe should express a unanimous consensus. This can only be arrived at by long discussion among all members. Any attempt to pressure leads to almost automatic rejection of the proposal. They see the role of

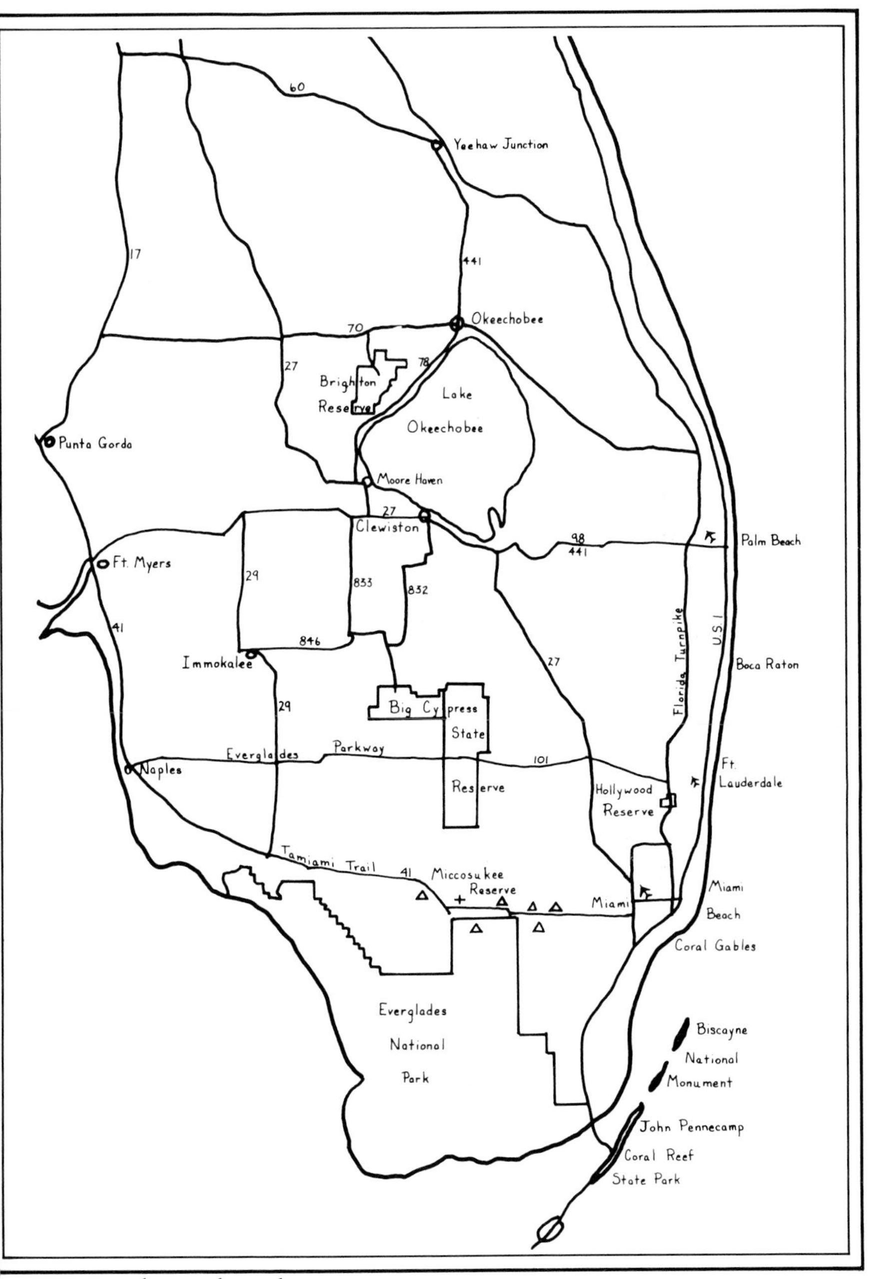

MAP 4. Seminole People Today

the leader as being one who can vigorously represent this consensus to outside institutions, the Agency, the state, county, or other threatening entities. If there ever was a need for dynamic, forceful leaders in the tribal past, it has been lost during the stage when they existed in small scattered camps. The Agency strongly desires energetic leaders who will rapidly push through the policies approved by the bureaucracy and see higher levels of education as a means of achieving that end. They also feel that higher levels of education will help produce these leaders considered necessary for their programs. The conflict in the two views of what a leader should be makes elective office of little value in the eyes of the tribal members. Education as a potential aid to service to fellow tribal members, however, may be a spur for some to seek more formal education.

THE FUTURE

As the Seminoles face the last quarter of the 20th century some highly probably changes can be foreseen with some degree of probability.

Population. While Seminole population has recovered to something less than what it was at the beginning of the American Period, it is unlikely that it will see any major increase as far as reservation residence is concerned. The provision of somewhat better public health, especially as this concerns survival of infants, mothers, and young children, has been largely responsible for the increases during this century. The provision of birth control pills will counter the population increase derived from the improved health measures. The fact that little opportunity for gainful employment on the reservations can be foreseen will mean that birth limitation and migration off the reservations will be highly effective means of limiting major growth.

ECONOMIC CONDITIONS

The cattle program will continue to be a major effort of many Indians on both Brighton and Big Cypress Reservations. The return from truck farms is probably as great, as is indicated by the fact that leasors of agricultural lands make a profit on a two-year lease which involves preparing the land and leaving it in permanent pasture. Cattle raising, however, is attractive to many Indians as it offers work in the open, near home, and has a romantic connotation. The Bureau of Indian Affairs also seems to strongly favor the cattle program at the expense of other uses of the limited land resources. After the dispersal of the tribally owned herd to individuals in 1954, the thrust has been consistently in the direction of larger individual herds. The limited amount of improved range available means that grazing fees have increased. Both the cattle experts of the University of Florida Cattle

Experiment Station and the Agency seem convinced that cattle herding on improved pasture is the highest use that can be made of the reservation lands. They also maintain that a minimum economically sound herd is 200 head. These statements seem to be based on the experience of white, free enterprise cattle ranches rather than on considerations of tribal Indian groups. The fact that the university-based experts have been able to demonstrate the sound financial gain of such large herds has strengthened the concept of cattle owning as a sound economic venture. What it will mean is that the large cattle owners will continue to be the major voice in the Cattlemen's Association and the corporation as they are the only ones who attend meetings and vote.

Improvements in breeds and management techniques can be expected to continue, assuring a higher rate of return to those owners with more than 200 head. Expansion of the total herd will involve the conversion of more land to improved pasture. This will mean that available capital will continue to be tied up in the pasture program and not be readily available for other enterprises. It is likely that the continued expansion of the cattle industry will lead to at least the beginnings of a class division on the reservation. The successful cattlemen will become the economically and politically dominant group, while the lower economic stratum will continue to find work in the vegetable fields, making craft objects, or will move off the reservation.

The success of activities related to the tourist business will probably continue to be a factor in the economy, simply because so much of South Florida is oriented toward this business. The production of craft souvenirs, however, does not result in high income levels, even when the tribe engages in the retail aspects, as it does at Hollywood and along the Tamiami Trail. Stoop labor in the vegetable fields will probably continue to be a major source of income. While the agricultural industry is making strenuous efforts to mechanize itself, there will always be a relative abundance of low paying jobs. Should current efforts at unionization be successful, pay scales will rise and working conditions improve. The subtropical climate should guarantee that South Florida will continue to raise a large part of the nation's vegetables. The only major threat is that uncontrolled drainage schemes will destroy the water table on which the productivity of the land depends. It seems clear that the danger is sufficiently evident that protective measures will be taken in time. The increasing access by the new cross-state road, Everglades Parkway, will probably increase both the availability of jobs and tourist opportunities. Neither tourism or farm labor seems likely to produce any appreciable rise in personal income.

Education. It seems likely that formal education in the county schools, special summer programs on the reservations, community college in nearby Miami, and eventually university education will become more common as the Seminoles can find ways in which skills acquired in school have some personal or tribal advantage. At present one Seminole girl has graduated from business college and at least one young man has attended the University of Florida. The need for trained personnel in the tribal enterprises will certainly stimulate longer education.

Religion. Christianity is definitely the course that the Seminoles will follow more and more completely. The old religious ceremonies are virtually extinct and there seems no pressure to revive them even in highly modified forms. The medicinemen will continue to find a place in the reservation society, however, as they fill a need not answered by the formal medicine provided in the clinics. The long training necessary for learning the arts of the medicinemen, however, presents a special problem of replacing the few elderly men who now have these skills. The increasing gap between the generations makes recruitment of new healers difficult.

Migration. Movement off the reservation seems certain to be increasingly a solution for the many problems that face the Indians. Florida is the most rapidly growing state east of

Courtesy Smithsonian Institution National Anthropological Archives

:MINOLE MAN (INGRAHAM CHARLIE) showing the use of carved wooden ball sticks Jack Tigertail's Camp, 1910. Stickball, the ancestor of modern lacrosse, was ayed by most Indians in the Eastern United States. Most tribes used wooden sticks ith a small netted pocket at the end. These carved wooden sticks seem to be ıique to the Seminole. The game had ritual overtones and was played between ams of all available men of one town against another town. It served in a very real nse to reduce other forms of rivalry and tension between groups. Betting was :avy at the games and violence often occurred.

Arizona and South Florida is already feeling the pinch of too many new migrants. Thus migration to Miami and the other cities of the east coast will be increasingly difficult. Lacking any training in the skills necessary for urban jobs, the Seminoles who want to migrate may find this increasingly difficult. At the same time the Everglades are the only open areas adjacent to the highly urbanized coastal strip. It is likely that some industry and especially recreational jobs will continue to spread westward and provide openings for Seminole workers adjacent to the reservations.

Factionalism. The Seminoles have developed an unknown number of factions. Recently the separation of the Miccosuki Tribe from the Seminole Tribe is a formalization of a long standing factional split. Conservative and progressive factions in the sense of being willing to adopt patterns of the general population are already present. Probably this trend will continue as the division between cattlemen and non-cattle owners grows more marked; because of the patterns of leadership there seems to be no real mechanism for reducing factionalism.

Indianness. Because the Seminoles, perhaps more than any other Indian people, have for a hundred and fifty years prized their right to be left alone, to be isolated from the culture of white America, it is probable that this deep seated value will not disappear overnight. Today the Seminoles are more aware than ever before of the luxuries of the non-Indian world just outside their remote reservations. Radio, television, and attendance at unsegregated public schools, all combine to create wants that cannot be supplied by traditional reservation life. The young Seminole are especially attracted to these values and the breakdown of the traditionally strong family camp leaves them with little knowledge of the old ways. Not yet participants in the present, they are adrift from the past. The result has been a serious rise in juvenile delinquincy. The very agencies that create their wants, however, also bring them news of the rising force of Pan-Indianism and of Red Power. These current concerns of the less isolated Indian tribes have not yet made much noticeable headway among the Seminoles. Participation in the Indian Claims cases and sporadic visits by Oklahoma Seminoles do, however, make the Florida Indians aware of the tidal movements among many American Indians. It seems certain that the Seminoles will be drawn into the Pan-Indian movement gathering power in Washington and at Wounded Knee. As long as young Seminoles proudly wear the distinctive patchwork jackets and skirts, so long will they be aware of their Indian and Seminole heritages.

SUGGESTED READINGS

The Seminoles remain probably the least known Indian tribe in the United States and the literature about them is scant. This list emphasizes the books and articles that cover in greater detail the subjects discussed above. The Indian Oral History Program at the University of Florida has been collecting verbal statements by Seminoles, and by others who know them well, that express the Seminoles' own view of their history and present circumstances.

ANONYMOUS, *Seminole Patchwork.* American Hobbyist, Vol. 6, Nos. 1 & 2, pp. 3-18. Denver, Colo., 1959.

A how-to description of Seminole patchwork clothing designs.

BOYD, MARK F. *The Seminole War: Its Background and Onset.* Florida Historical Quarterly, Vol. 30, No. 1, pp. 3-115. Gainesville, Florida 1951.

Well documented and written account of the origins of the Second Seminole War.

CAPRON, LOUIS. *The Medicine Bundles of the Florida Seminole and the Green Corn Dance.* Bureau of American Ethnology, Bulletin No. 151, Anthropological Paper No. 35, pp. 155-210. Washington, D.C., 1953.

The first description of the sacred bundles and how they are used by the medicinemen.

COHEN, M. M. *Notices of Florida and the Campaigns,* with Introduction by O. Z. Typer, Jr. Gainesville, Florida, University of Florida Press, 1964.

A facsimile of the 1836 edition with a modern introduction. Describes the early events of the Second Seminole War.

DENSMORE, FRANCES. *Seminole Music.* Bureau of American Ethnology, Bulletin, No. 161, Washington, D.C. 1956.

A detailed presentation and discussion of Seminole music by the principal student of American Indian music.

GARBARINO, MERWYN S., *Big Cypress, A Changing Seminole Community.* New York: Holt, Rinehart, and Winston, 1972.

A sensitively written description of Big Cypress in modern times with special attention to the cattle program and the problems of Seminole leadership.

GOGGIN, JOHN M., Ed. *Osceola.* Florida Historical Quarterly, Vol. 33, Nos. 3 & 4. Gainesville, 1955.

Contains articles by Goggin, Ward, Coe, Sturtevant, Porter, Neill, and Boyd on various aspects of the life of Osceola.

MACCAULEY, CLAY. *The Seminole Indians of Florida.* Bureau of American Ethnology, Annual Report, No. 5, pp. 469-531. Washington, D.C. 1887.

The first scientific description of the Seminole in modern times.

MAHON, JOHN K. *History of the Second Seminole War.* Gainesville, Florida: University of Florida Press, 1967.

A brillant study by a modern historian of the most important of the Seminole wars.

WILSON, MINNIE MOORE. *The Seminoles of Florida.* New York, Moffat, Yard & Co. 1896.

The earliest popular book on the Seminoles by someone who lived near them for many years. Had many editions and served to popularize these Indians for many people.

CHARLES H. FAIRBANKS, Professor of Anthropology at the University of Florida in Gainesville, has carried out extensive archeological and ethnohistorical research on the Indians of the Southeastern United States. He was formerly Chairman of the Department of Anthropology at the University of Florida, and has taught at Florida State University and Mercer University.

Fairbanks has conducted research in prehistoric and historic cultures for the National Park Service at Ocmulgee National Monument and at Ft. Frederica National Monument. He is currently directing archeological excavations at St. Simon's Island, Georgia, and in St. Augustine, Florida.